DEATH
ON A SUMMER'S DAY

DEATH
ON A SUMMER'S DAY

THE TRUE STORY OF THE MURDER BRITAIN WATCHED ON LIVE TELEVISION

DAVID BLACKIE

JOHN BLAKE

Published by John Blake Publishing Ltd.

3, Bramber Court, 2 Bramber Road,
London W14 9PB, England

www.blake.co.uk

First published in Hardback in 2006

ISBN 1 84454 190 8

British Library Cataloguing-in-Publication Data:

A catalogue record for this book is available from the British Library.

Design by www.envydesign.co.uk

Printed in Great Britain by Creative Print and Design

1 3 5 7 9 10 8 6 4 2

Papers used by John Blake Publishing are natural, recyclable products
made from wood grown in sustainable forests. The manufacturing processes
conform to the environmental regulations of the country of origin.

Every attempt has been made to contact the relevant copyright-holders,
but some were unobtainable. We would be grateful if the appropriate people
could contact us.

This book is dedicated all those ordinary, unknown and unsung police officers who regularly put their careers and their lives on the line every time they pick up a gun.

CONTENTS

Foreword	ix
Chapter 1	1
Chapter 2	7
Chapter 3	25
Chapter 4	41
Chapter 5	53
Chapter 6	77
Chapter 7	77
Chapter 8	91
Chapter 9	109
Chapter 10	129
Chapter 11	143
Chapter 12	157

Chapter 13   181

Chapter 14   207

Chapter 15   221

Chapter 16   239

Chapter 17   257

Chapter 18   263

Chapter 19   273

Epilogue   285

Appendix   289

FOREWORD

I first formed the idea to write this book after leaving the police service. I thought long and hard about my motives for doing so, and it is accurate to say that these have changed considerably during the exercise. While conducting research for this book I interviewed many people, some of whom have had their lives turned upside-down by the events described herein; for some, the gunman will chase them through their dreams. Then there were those who, for their own individual reasons, refused to speak to me at all. To others, it felt as if I was almost their father confessor, so eager were they to share their experiences. But of all these, Dryden was the one person, the enigma, whom I felt that I had to see.

Some of the people mentioned within this book have since died, but none so tragically as Harry Collinson, who perished in an unnecessary confrontation between two human beings that was to have such dire consequences for so many people: children deprived of a father, a sister deprived of a brother. Many others will have suffered in many ways. This book is not intended to be an accounting, a witch hunt, but rather a tale from which salutary lessons must be learned to ensure that such stupidity should never be repeated. Nonetheless, I regretfully remain assured that the fallibility of man will allow a senseless imitation of such waste.

I could not have completed this work without the help and encouragement of others. My purpose in writing this book was to create a better understanding not only of what happened but also of its effects on others, myself included, and I hope that those not directly involved in the history of events portrayed here – whether known, unknown or still dear to me but nonetheless touched by these events – may also understand. I must therefore pay tribute to the support that was given to me by all those who have contributed to the book, especially my friend and confidant Ian Wriglesworth; to the assistance of a truly remarkable police officer, Arthur Proud; and to the unstinting encouragement and total trust of my dear wife, Carol, whose support was unwavering, even when times were bad.

ONE

*B*one-tired − a strange expression, but one I now understood exactly. I was so mentally and physically exhausted that my bones ached.

Bone-tired.

I held the key between forefinger and thumb, the last rays of the still-warm spring sun glinting on the dull brass. Pausing for a moment, my hand shaking slightly, and trying hard to focus, I gathered myself before crossing yet another boundary. I really had crossed enough bloody boundaries that day, not to mention ditches and fields. Trying to make as little noise as possible, I slid the key carefully into the lock and heard the tumblers fall as the door eased open. I thought that my day was finished; I didn't, *couldn't* imagine what was yet to come.

I closed the door softly behind me, placed my heavy kit

bag, which had travelled everywhere with me, gratefully on the floor and opened the door into the living room. I was totally exhausted by the day's events but, before I could even register the image in front of me, I was assaulted with a barrage of noise from my three children, who were sitting with their mother on the sofa, facing the flickering monitor in the corner, which was replaying the day's events. I half-thought I could see my own face on the screen. Or was it just a reflection?

'Daddy! Daddy!'

Those were the two words that reverberated through my brain: 'Daddy! Daddy!' I knew that I was home, but in my head I was still there.

'Daddy! Daddy!'

Please, please, for God's sake, shut up!

'Mrs Collinson's son's been shot.'

I heard the words, but my brain refused to register them, refused to *believe* them. I turned around slowly to see on the television scenes in which I'd played a part just a few short hours earlier. Everything was in slow motion; I couldn't seem to get my mind to work properly. Was it a TV drama or was it reality? Everything blurred and I found myself unable to distinguish fact from fiction. I couldn't remember. But I *had* been there. I didn't need to see it on TV; I'd seen it with my own eyes.

But I'd missed it! I'd overlooked one crucial piece of information that would turn the day's events into something personal.

'Daddy! Daddy! Mrs Collinson's son's been shot.'

2

I could almost hear the crack of the gun as the last piece of the jigsaw – if that's what it was – fell into place. *Mrs Collinson's son's been shot.* And I'd been there. Slowly, the awful truth dawned on me. How could I not have known?

I was so proud of being the ultimate professional, always striving to prove myself. It had all been part of my job, and of course no one could do it better, could they? A man had died that day, and I was doing what I had to do to rescue an awful situation. I had stood over his corpse, the body of this man I didn't know. I wasn't interested in him as a person, a human being; he was a case study, an objective problem to be solved, and I'd been so full of myself.

I had known him, all right, this bleeding piece of meat. In another place, another context, I had known him. True, I'd known him only as Mrs Collinson's son, but Mrs Collinson was our next-door neighbour and she was known to me, to all our family. She was a neat old lady with whom I would exchange pleasantries and who would sometimes look disgruntled when my kids kicked a football into her garden but who would still buy them sweets at Christmas. This woman had a son – three sons, in fact.

I remembered him now; he'd been a man with whom I'd exchanged the time of day. He wasn't a man now, was he? That anonymous corpse had once been a man, a human being, not a bloody tactical objective.

I didn't need to look at the television. I'd seen the aftermath. I'd seen it all, and I'd heard it all. I had been –

3

God help me – a part of it all. The children had seen the images at a distant remove, sterile, and they would hopefully never have to deal with such grisly reality – at least, not if I could help it. All of a sudden, I had an overwhelming need to protect them. I looked at my wife and saw comprehension in her eyes. She knew where I'd been that day, but she didn't understand. She would never understand. That day, there was nobody who could understand.

Guilt surged within me. I wanted to be sick. I had an obligation to purge myself and speak to my neighbour. What had I done? What had I not done? I knew only that I had to apologise, but for what? For not recognising her son? Wordlessly, like an automaton, I turned away from my wife and children and walked back out of the front door, back out into the forgiving yet accusing sunlight, turned and walked the few yards to her door. This was not reality. I couldn't believe I was doing this.

I gently knocked and the door opened. A tall, broad and ruddy woman who looked sturdy enough to withstand shocks like this stood there, tear-stained. She was the wife of another of my neighbour's sons, one who was still alive, but even she was showing the strain of the day. She looked at me with empty eyes and I could find no words.

'I am so sorry. I'm so very, very sorry.'

I felt like I was carrying the burden of guilt upon my shoulders for the loss of her brother-in-law. Common sense told me that it wasn't my fault, but I still felt like it was, for I knew that those tears need never have been shed and this awful grief could have been avoided.

Again, 'I'm sorry.'

She mouthed some form of thanks. I couldn't say what, exactly. I looked at her beseechingly. 'Anything. Anything at all,' I said lamely.

She knew what I meant, but she didn't know what I could do, and neither did I. I could never make up for not recognising my next-door neighbour's son as he lay before me, three bullets in his lifeless body.

Our eyes met again. It felt as though she was probing deep into my soul, trying to find some answers to the inevitable questions, and the guilt burned in me as she saw that I had none. She nodded her thanks and the door closed silently again in front of me. I just stood there, unable to move. It seemed as if a cloud had descended and enshrouded that cottage – the cottage of an elderly lady with only two sons now – with grief.

I was shaking. I stood outside the cottage for a moment longer, trying to gulp air into my lungs. I knew that it would take the people inside a long time to heal. I knew, too, that it would take me a long time. This, I knew, was the beginning of a journey for me. There would be many words – some in anger, many in sorrow. There would be many questions, too, as well as many recriminations and some sympathy. I couldn't see where it would go. I couldn't even guess where it might end.

I gathered myself together and went home for the second time that day, knowing that I'd soon be facing a barrage of questions from my chattering children. As I entered the house, my wife stood at the kitchen door, her solemn brown eyes upon me, accusing. What had I brought into the house? But she asked me no questions. She feared the answers.

However, I needed answers. There would be questions that, on the surface, might appear comparatively simple, but the truth ran deep. Those questions might be answered one day, but there would always remain those that I would ask of myself. Would I ever get any answers to these?

'Daddy! Daddy! Mrs Collinson's son's been shot!'

TWO

Durham and Northumberland, where this history takes place, are two of the most sparsely populated counties in England and, because of the distances between them and, in some cases, their isolation, all the cities, towns and villages have their own fiercely defended individual identities. Call someone from Sunderland a Geordie, for instance, and you're likely to cause a fistfight.

The smaller villages are just as proud of their own heritage, none more so than the town of Chopwell, also known as 'Little Moscow' – and with good reason. If Napoleon had retreated from Chopwell in the winter, his troops would have foundered in snow and cold by the time they'd got five miles down the road. But it wasn't for its weather that the town won its nickname. It was derived during the General Strike of 1926, a time when the tentacles of fomenting industrial unrest had stretched west from Newcastle to the towns and villages beyond. According to one of the contemporary local politicians, 'Chopwell is a city set on a hill that cannot be hid.'

Many saw the new socialism that was sweeping through the region as being a direct response to the evils of the First World War. Indeed, today in the Northeast there's scarcely a town or village or even just a scar of miners' cottages on a remote hillside that doesn't have a market square or main street that's dominated by a well-cared-for memorial to the fallen who sacrificed their lives in that conflict. Patriotic duty blighted many families in the North-East who readily gave up their sons to do their duty for king and country, but their bloody sacrifice seemed to gain nothing but poverty and despair for the common people of the region. Many there saw the new wave of social change as a cure to all their tribulations.

In fact, there was still plenty of money in the area, but it was concentrated in the hands of a few who saw this new battle-cry of socialism as a Communist plague that had to be quickly stamped out before it consumed them and their way of life. The majority of people in the Northeast were wholly occupied with scraping out a meagre living, with men, women and children working in grime and dirt for twelve or more hours a day while the lucky few sat on their well-covered backsides in panelled offices, living off the misery of their workers.

One could be forgiven for assuming that political awareness wasn't at the top of the agenda in most households at that time, yet this couldn't be further from the truth, as discontent was bubbling up all over the region leading to strikes, walkouts, violence and even riot.

This was certainly the case in Chopwell, a community of 3,000 souls described in the *Northern Mail* at that time as being 'known far and wide as the reddest village in England'. According to a local political activist, 'The only thing that differentiates [Chopwell] from other towns is that it is a little bit higher in intelligence and in outlook than most of the other towns.' Indeed, when sentencing fifty offenders from the town for rioting during the 1926 strike, the magistrate told them, 'Why you and those associated with you don't go to Russia, I don't know. We don't want you. Nobody wants you. You're just a source of danger to the community.' The people of Chopwell were rightly proud of their heritage, and their determination and grit was a characteristic attribute of the inhabitants of the North-East.

It was at Chopwell that the Collinson family had their home and where their story really began, with James and his brother, John, who in 1920 decided to begin their own haulage business, starting out with just one broken-down old lorry that was sufficient to carry road stone, the by-product of local mining interests. This was a brave step at the time, setting out to become entrepreneurs when wealth was the preserve of the few. Nevertheless, the business prospered (although not at any great rate), allowing the brothers to purchase two more vehicles.

Both James and John held strong (and not always the

same) views about politics, but both were united in their support for the region's burgeoning socialism and objected vociferously to what they saw as England's unnecessary involvement in a second European war. Exempt as they were from military service by reason of their age and occupation, both brothers continued to build their business. Work was plentiful, as transport was needed to fulfil much-needed government contracts, with which the brothers could boost their income without, seemingly, over-compromising their political viewpoints.

James, the elder of the two, had by this time married Mabel, who had provided him with three strong and vigorous sons: Eric in 1930, Frank in 1933 and Roy in 1939. The family thrived and prospered until the end of the war, when the bottom fell out of the haulage trade as a result of increased competition and the scarcity of business. It turned out that there wasn't enough money in the business for both brothers to earn a living, and they decided to part company, professionally.

The Collinsons were originally of farming stock, and James and Mabel, seeing the writing on the wall, took the little that was their share of the company and returned with their three children to what they knew best. They moved to Home Farm in Edmundbyers, County Durham, which wasn't that far from Chopwell but nevertheless might as well have been on the moon, exposed as it was on the remote moorland hillside. It was there that the couple's fourth and last child, Harry, was born in 1945.

There was, in fact, an awful geographical irony to

Harry's birth, as it would not be far from Edmundbyers that he would eventually meet his untimely death, at the hands of a man who had also been born close by.

One of Harry's brothers described the pace of life during their childhood in Edmundbyers as 'the last of the summer wine', although it's debatable whether this appreciation was realistic or coloured by a romantic hindsight of idyllic sunsets over blasted heaths, the gentle noises of the livestock, the smell of home baking wafting across the farmyard, tempting in the family and their workers at the end of the day. Harry was welcomed into the house, but he was yet another mouth to feed, and his presence put pressure on an already extended family budget. The children were forced to share bedrooms, and Roy and Harry – the two youngest – bunked down together. However, they found that the six years between them proved to be an intolerable gap, especially at their tender years, and Roy gravitated more towards his elder brothers, Eric and Frank, who slept in the next-door bedroom. They were his role models and the brothers he really wanted to play with, while Harry was considered an intruder into their gang and was hence isolated from the other three brothers almost from birth. He was, it seemed, destined to be on his own, and so it was predictable that his life would take a different path to that of his brothers.

Casual labourers came and went on the farm, but by and large the family led a pretty lonely existence. The farmhouse's spare bedroom was occupied by a female farm worker, and at that stage in their development she was in all likelihood an object of interest and fantasy for the older boys. However, their rural idyll wasn't a bed of roses; it was also hard work, sweat and graft. All the family, even young Harry, were expected to pitch in and help, especially with the seasonal work. One particular year, when Harry was about four years old, all of the family members pitched in with the haymaking, which as well as being hard work spawned some fun and games out in the fresh air and sunshine. In quick succession, a series of calamities befell the boys: Eric fell off a horse and broke his collarbone, Roy broke his leg, and Harry – not to be outdone – managed to nip his fingers in the bailer, resulting in three out of the four Collinson children ending up in nearby Shotley Bridge Hospital together.

The boys would spend the majority of their time around the farm, making their own amusement, largely because money was tight but also because, in those days, people seldom travelled. The three eldest boys played happily enough together, but Harry was generally left out of their games. There were very few children of his age left in the village, and most of those that were there were girls, a species as yet a mystery to him. Harry therefore didn't have the opportunities to cause mayhem and mischief around the farm and village that his elder brothers had, and so he grew up a rather different sort of child to his siblings, more studious and somewhat withdrawn. He developed an absorbing passion for nature, holding a particular interest in farming. He would grow seeds and cuttings, marvelling at how they could mature and ripen as spring turned to summer.

At the age of eight, like thousands of other boys his age, Harry collected conkers. He took his best, most rounded conker and, instead of spoiling it with a hole for string to prepare for encounters in the school playground, he dug a small hole in the soil and planted the seed within sight of his house, then nurtured it as it grew and flourished under his stubborn care. The tree that sprang from it still stands today, over fifty years on, spreading its shade over the rear garden of Home Farm at Edmundbyers.

Scattered amongst the farms in the village were a number of derelict old buses and caravans that were used as farm workers' accommodation and holiday spots for local people from Shotley Bridge. People would use them to stay for weekends in order to enjoy the pleasures of the countryside. However, the building of the nearby Derwent Reservoir at the end of the 1950s would change forever the tranquil, sparsely populated countryside around Edmundbyers. The hovels were cleared away to make way for a purpose-built, sterile and functional caravan site, established to accommodate workers on the reservoir from as far away as Wallsend and Newcastle. With it came more cars, television and electricity for all the residents of the area. With sure, firm strokes, the new technology of the latter half of the twentieth century was painted on to the rural canvas of the North-East. With such developments came new opportunities – opportunities that had passed Harry's brothers by but that would take him into the professional classes.

All of Harry's brothers would accept, without equivocation, that Harry Collinson was more intelligent than they were. He had always maintained a responsible attitude to his studies, concentrating on his homework even when the sun blazed down on the fields. It almost goes without saying that, when he took his Eleven Plus examination, he sailed through without any difficulty, whereupon he was granted a place at the grammar school at Consett, where he easily gained the O- and A-levels he needed in order to embark on the next stage in his career. He was viewed as a model child by other local parents, who considered him a respectable and clever boy, and was even asked to chaperone one local family's young daughter (with whom he would later work) on the grammar-school bus.

In 1955, when Harry was ten years old, the family was hit when father James left home without warning to set up home with a female companion down south, in Welwyn Garden City. This left Mabel and her four sons to run the farm, and it's a credit to Mabel's determination that she managed to carry on. Little more was heard of her errant husband, who returned to the North-East only briefly in 1983, when he was severely ill, seeing his sons for one last, somewhat acrimonious visit before he died two years later.

The change in circumstances that James's departure had brought about forced some adjustments at Home Farm. Money had already been tight and with the head of the household *in absentia* finances became even tighter, so to supplement the family income Roy went to work at the Consett Iron Company. (It's conceivable that he might even have met a man named Albert Dryden there.) His two brothers Eric and Frank, meanwhile, left the farm to fulfil their National Service, from which they eventually returned home safe and sound. At about the time that his brothers returned, Roy departed to join the Royal Marines, and, when he in turn was discharged, he took various jobs, eventually working his way back to Edmundbyers from the south of England. He then married and took over Three Bridges Farm at Stocksfield, where he and his wife raised two children and where he farms to this day.

By this time, Eric and Frank were both back in the field, too, Eric having taken over the farm at Edmundbyers and Frank purchasing a farm nearby, just outside Wolsingham, by Tunstall Reservoir. With Mabel now on her own but maintaining her fierce independence, the boys persuaded her to move to a cottage in Wolsingham that nestled cosily down in the dale.

Meanwhile, Harry had moved on from grammar school to the prestigious Newcastle University, the first in his family to progress to higher education. His interests had changed little by this time, and as he'd always harboured a keen interest in environment matters, long before such studies became fashionable, he decided to read for a degree in Town Planning, a science then still in its infancy.

By the time he arrived at university, Harry had already mapped out his goals and, indeed, his future, in his usual methodical and analytical manner. He knew that he wanted to work in local government as a planner, to take his part in improving the environment and shaping the future. As he'd grown up, he'd become more principled, perhaps picking up on the social history of his birthplace. (His father and his father's family had always been seen as somewhat left wing by the local community.) Already holding socialist leanings, his views became more radical while at university, but, rather than being rooted in an ideal of pure political socialism, Harry's were more egalitarian, social principles. However, his brothers didn't share his robustly held views, and this led to some lively family debates. Roy recalled, 'We used to have some real ding-dong arguments when Harry came home at weekends. He thought that these people out of the slum areas of Newcastle, if you took them out of those areas and housed them in nice new estates, they would automatically become better people. He always thought the best of everybody, really. He used to stick up for the underdog, as he used to call them.'

The brothers saw themselves as realists and, as they were living in the commercial world of farming, it could be argued (and Harry frequently did) that, in their own way, they were supporting the building blocks of capitalism. His support for what they saw as lame-duck causes never left him.

For the most part, Harry supported himself through university, receiving only limited financial help from his family, taking small jobs here and there to supplement his grant. Never a spendthrift, he even managed to acquire a series of cars – never smart ones – which he cared for with almost religious fervour. When he came home for weekends, his first job was always to clean his current vehicle, to wash off the dirt of the city – a city that he perhaps saw himself rebuilding.

In the 1960s, attitudes towards town planning changed. The politicians, both national and regional, had taken over from private enterprise, seeking to regulate the planning process, to introduce standards, hopefully doing what was the best for society. Planning policy came to determine the environmental evolution of the nation, becoming an exercise in wholesale social engineering. Government was determining that this was the way people would live in the future, that it was for their own benefit. This philosophy appealed to Harry, who found it difficult to accept that some people didn't want to live in tower blocks, to have their roads straightened, to have their unsanitary terraced houses knocked down. The relentless march of progress had a certain logic to it that appealed to the pedant in him.

While he was at university, Harry found his first love, a waiflike girl named Susan who stole his heart. Their romance blossomed and they married as soon as Harry got his degree.

Almost immediately after graduating, Harry was offered a job as an assistant planner with Norwich City Council and he and Susan moved south. However, the flat fens of Norfolk were a far cry from the hills and dales of Durham, which he missed painfully. For a while, Harry and Susan were happy and the marriage prospered, but things turned sour when Susan soon became bored and fell for Harry's boss, Norwich's chief planning officer. Their affair was at first clandestine, but it soon reached a pitch where Susan decided to leave the unfortunate Harry and set up home with his superior. This wrecked Harry, who was understandably bitter and distraught, as were both his and Susan's families. As well as losing his wife, he had been placed in a ridiculously untenable job situation. He was forced to move back home.

In 1971, Harry became a planning officer for Durham County Council, involving himself with formulating policy for the future development of the county. This wasn't really what he wanted to do; he wanted to deal with real people and their aspirations, which he believed were the fundamentals of town planning, the control of development that would ensure the best future for the environment. He immersed himself in his work, adhering rigidly to his principles. He determined that he would do what he could: he would create greenery out of slag dust; he would generate housing on derelict factory land. He saw far beyond just bricks and mortar.

Harry valued his independence and bought a house in Durham, near Neville's Cross, which had been the scene of one of the great battles of the English Civil War. In order to be able to afford his mortgage, he needed to supplement his income and so decided to take in lodgers. As an ancient university town, Durham had a large student population, so he had little difficulty in finding occupants for his spare rooms. As it turned out, one of those who came to stay didn't leave.

Ann was a student at the local university and the daughter of an aeroplane designer, and Harry fell in love with and eventually married her. The couple were soon blessed with two children, Katie and Robert. While becoming a good father and husband, however, Harry still lived for his work.

Harry's colleagues had noticed a gradual change in him; he had developed what has been described as an 'attitude'. It seemed that he felt it was his responsibility to put right all the wrong decisions that had gone before and were blighting proper social engineering. The further he progressed in his career, the more marked this attitude became.

Harry's area of responsibility was the consideration, assessment and recommendations for planning applications of all development within the council's purview. His was a controversial role, and local feeling about individual planning proposals often ran high, but Harry had never been one to shy away from controversy and would often come into conflict with applicants and objectors alike. Within the constraints of local policies, Harry was quite capable of imposing his own views and making his own rules

In 1974, local government in England and Wales underwent a restructuring, which ultimately meant that there were jobs aplenty to be had in the public sector. Harry, like many, saw this as an opportunity to move onwards and upwards, and he left Durham County Council to work for the Derwentside District Council. Derwentside was at the time a predominantly rural area that included the town of Consett, where the council offices were located. Such district councils were coming of age, being given more responsibility and carrying out their own planning functions, and Harry Collinson felt like he was coming home. It was in this role that he really saw his future, shaping the environment he had known as a child and improving the lives of the people he cared about.

Derwentside District Council covered an area of high unemployment with severely underfunded public facilities and housing stock, and Harry saw his new role as an opportunity to put his social principles to work. Mike Bonser joined the council at the same time as Harry (he remembered Harry at that stage in his career as 'studious, precise and a stickler for detail') and was the clerk to the planning committee, so from the outset the two worked together closely.

There's always a suspicion that, in local government, the political power is held by just a few people, and this was certainly the case in Derwentside. Some have said that at the time there was no real democracy within the council, which did not sit well with Harry, who found it hard to work effectively within those surroundings and was compelled to appear to modify his opinions. Dealing with everyone fairly, he encountered large firms and individual applicants both on a totally professional level, although individuals with a problem were more likely to be treated with consideration and a cup of tea. He stuck to his policies and principles, holding strong views about right and wrong; he would give correct advice but would, necessarily, always abide by decisions of the elected members, even if he personally disagreed. Many respected him for such integrity, but some did not.

Harry never took well to people or organisations that he saw as trying to buck the system or challenge his own professional opinion to further their own ends (there are numerous stories of Harry getting involved in confrontations and arguments). However, he could also be fickle. On one particular housing estate built in Shotley Bridge, Harry had insisted, despite protestations from the developer, that the houses should be built from a particular type of pale brick. Two years later, after they had been built, he was heard to say, 'Terrible bricks, those. I don't know why we allowed them.' A member of his staff remembered one particular application for the construction of a garage that would virtually be hidden from public view by a neighbouring building. The applicant wanted to build the garage with breezeblocks, but Harry insisted that it be made of stone, which would make it altogether more expensive. On this occasion, another member of staff mediated in the affair, with the result that half of the garage was stone-clad (in case it might be seen from the road) while the other half was naked breezeblock.

By this time, the girl whom he had chaperoned on the bus to school many, many years earlier, Helen Winter, was also a planner and had worked alongside Harry. As she remembered, his overriding concern was to conserve the environment. He accepted the need for development but felt that it could not take place at the cost of the local surroundings. He was always prepared for robust debate, but he was also known to sulk sometimes if he didn't get his own way.

A more serious consequence of Harry's value judgements in the control of development was the almost total boycott by major house-builders of the Derwentside area during the early 1980s. This embargo was openly accepted to be the consequence of Harry's attitude towards these national firms and what he saw as their disregard of good planning. He was severely taken to task over this state of affairs by his superiors, however, and after this some saw him as more discerning and understanding.

While there might have been a change in his attitudes, Harry was still so engrossed in his work that once again his personal life suffered. He and his wife, Ann, grew apart and were eventually divorced, after which Harry stayed in the house in Durham while Ann moved with the children to Beverley, where she later married a prison chaplain. If Harry's work had been his primary interest before, it now consumed him.

Helen Winter was working alongside Harry at Derwentside by this time, and she spoke of him fondly as 'a caring person, not a possessions person, who made you feel guilty about having a big car or not taking enough interest in the environment'. Some, however, considered him a bit wacky; builders and developers would bring brick samples into the offices, and Harry saved these up and used them to build walls. Meanwhile, he came up with a novel rust-prevention scheme for his old Sunbeam car – his pride and joy – that involved pop-riveting fertiliser bags underneath the wheel arches.

By now, Harry was almost classed as an eccentric. Not at all concerned with his own wardrobe, he was described as a 'tailor's nightmare'. Every Saturday, he ran a second-hand clothes stall in Durham marketplace, the proceeds of which he donated to charities. He was usually to be found there at weekends, rain or shine, doing his best to sell as much as he could. He would grow despondent on days when sales were slow, but he was prepared to give up his time and his own money for such good causes as a practical demonstration of his beliefs, making his own contribution in his own, highly individual way. Not a natural social animal, Harry nonetheless would make the effort and would turn up at staff leaving parties, even holding parties at his house for the students who were staying with him.

Harry's life changed when he met Caroline Mason, a lecturer at the university who was his intellectual equal and would later be described as an extremely dignified woman by Chief Inspector Arthur Proud. They had similar interests and both loved walking in the Lake District. Caroline had her own house in Durham and got on well with Harry's children. Many would later say that, if it hadn't been for the tragic turn of events that occurred later, they might well have become a family together. Harry began to open up, and some remember him during this time as being extremely good company. This period saw the birth of an easier Harry, a man more comfortable with himself.

THREE

It's about a steady ten-minute drive from Edmundbyers, Harry Collinson's birthplace, to the town of Consett, which provides the traveller with an opportunity to contemplate the beauties of nature – the open moorland, the pasture and, in between, the bursts of dense woodland that, in late spring, are full of the aroma of wild garlic and the azure haze of bluebells.

In contrast, Consett in the previous century was a place of strong men and silent women, both seemingly cast from the molten metal that was the lifeblood of the town. A pall of red dust that hung permanently over the town discoloured hanging washing and congested the lungs of the town's inhabitants. At one time, Consett was a vibrant piece of the industrial heartland of the North-East, but it was eventually abandoned in the 1980s as not being economically viable and forced to find its own salvation by regeneration, a long, slow process that seems to have flooded the town with cheap supermarkets and pubs and little else. Surprisingly enough, the people of the area seem to have maintained a quiet dignity in the face of their constant misfortune, and there is a tight sense of community that the outsider might find hard to penetrate.

Such was the case within the home of the Dryden family, a humble council house at 26 Priestman Avenue, The Grove, Consett, from whence came the other half of this fatal conjunction.

Albert Dryden was a child of fancifulness who became a man of contradictions. His existence would become a juggernaut of what might have been, what could have been, but very rarely what actually was. His childish fantasy would lead to adult fantasy, which in turn would give rise to his ultimate conviction that he was right in pursuing a cause that was nevertheless fatally flawed.

His parents were firm Salvationists and his mother Nora was very active in the Army. She was described by many as a saint, a wonderful little woman who never swore, never drank, never gave way to idle gossip and was always ready to help other people.

It is to Albert's eternal credit that he adored his mother and cared for her in her dotage, just as she had cared for him as a child. Meanwhile his father, also Albert, was the epitome of a northern patriarch, a strict, clean-living man who did his best to bring up his children straight and true through the good times and bad – and there were many of the latter.

Albert was born on 12 May 1940, a brother for Audrey, Leslie, Alan and Elsie, and Nora later bore three further children: Nora, George and Ann. Within the street in which they lived, they were always known as a happy family in their small house. Albert Sr doted on his children and was conscientious about providing for his family, keeping in work as much as he could, despite the fluctuating employment situation at his workplace, the Consett Iron Company. If he was laid off, he would take work wherever he could as it became available, on building sites or as a farm labourer, in order to put food on the table.

Albert Jr has mixed memories of his childhood, sometimes remembering that he mingled well with people of his own age and that he enjoyed playing football and cricket, although he was able to slip into a world of solitary imagination at will. He found satisfaction at an early age in hand-crafting playthings such as toy guns. While he was prepared to engage in team sports, he found individual events more to his liking. (Strangely, one of his bizarre recollections is of being the second-best javelin thrower in his school – a claim that perhaps can be related to his later assertion that he was the second-best pistol shot in England, a claim that has no basis in fact.) He is quite prepared to admit that he was not good at reading or writing or numbers, although he always counted gardening as an enjoyable activity.

One of Albert Jr's favourite pastimes, however, was going on picnics, with either his family or just down to the woods with a slice of bread and jam and his friends. He also looked forward to two special trips out each year: one with the ladies of the Women's Institute, which was a somewhat staid affair and conducted under the watchful eye of his mother, and an altogether more fun trip with his school mates to Whitley Bay, where they could clamber over the rocks, play the slot machines at the penny arcades and gorge themselves sick on sweets and ice creams.

When Albert started at the Grove Infant and Junior School in Consett, to say that he didn't enjoy the experience would be to understate things considerably. It took him a long time to accept the concept of formal education, if indeed he ever did. It wasn't that he didn't want to go to school, as such, but that he had so many other, more important things he wanted to do.

Elsie, one of his older sisters, described Albert as a very ordinary child but with a very determined streak that became apparent from a very early age. His eating habits, for instance, didn't fit in with those of the rest of the family, and he was fussy with his food, too, which frustrated his mother considerably when money was tight. Meanwhile, while his reading didn't improve, he had a dogged determination about him and would take a book (he especially enjoyed any book, magazine or comic about the Wild West) and sit for hours, reading word by word, trying to make sense of it all.

Albert's abiding interest in all things American would remain with him throughout his adult years, and it's highly likely that he would have loved to see himself as a frontiersman in later years. At every opportunity, he would escape to Taylor's Wood at the bottom of his garden to join his friends in fairly violent games of cowboys and Indians.

Although always getting into scrapes, whether at home or school, Albert would always manage to get out of them somehow, whether by guile or charm. Within his school, he wasn't by all accounts a very intelligent boy, although his teachers found him to be little real trouble. He was better at practical subjects, finding himself to be more adept at manufacturing bows and arrows and catapults for his boyhood games. He always attributed this interest in making things and his natural manual dexterity to an uncle who dabbled as a clockmaker and inventor and who had a local reputation as something of an eccentric. It's possible that this early influence contributed a great deal to Dryden's own later character.

At the age of eleven, Albert was sent to Consett Secondary Modern School, where he managed to endure the school system for a further four years. It was there that he was to experience one of the pivotal moments of his life, which was to have the most extreme effect upon him in the future. Soon after he started attending the school, a friend of his (whose identity he has never revealed) unknowingly initiated a tragic chain of events when he sidled up to Albert in the school playground and told him of a real cowboy gun that his father kept in a drawer at home. Albert's imagination was so excited by this revelation that he immediately insisted that he see it, pestering his friend to bring it to school.

The boy was infected by his friend's enthusiasm and agreed to bring it into school the next day. At lunchtime, he found Albert, who by this time was so animated at the prospect of actually being able to see and touch a real gun that he could hardly contain himself. Furtively, the boys crept into the toilets and, after making sure they were alone, locked themselves in a cubicle. Carefully, Albert's friend opened his satchel and drew out a parcel wrapped in grimy cloth, which he then slowly unwrapped, as if to tease Albert.

There, in the dimly lit boys' lavatories, Dryden saw his first glimpse of a real gun. It was a handgun, a pistol, a revolver – a real cowboy gun, gleaming dully on the cloth under a thin coating of oil. Almost reverentially, he picked it up, feeling the weight of the machined metal, relishing the sensation of the bulky butt in his adolescent palm. He'd read enough cowboy comics to understand its rudimentary workings, and mesmerised he pulled back the hammer with both thumbs until he heard it click into place, pointed it at an imaginary target, looked over the sights and slowly squeezed until the trigger snapped and the hammer fell on to an empty chamber.

It was a mystical, magical moment. For the first time in his life, Dryden felt the power that a gun could give him. There was no doubt in his mind that *this* was his gun. It was meant to be his gun. He had to have it. But would his friend part with it?

At first, Albert's friend was reluctant, fearing his father's wrath, but Albert wasn't easily dissuaded and asked him how much money he wanted for the weapon. Seeing how desperate Albert was to possess the pistol, the boy realised that he could name his own price, so they haggled and eventually agreed on a price of ten shillings (a great deal of money to a schoolboy in the 1950s), to be paid at the rate of sixpence a week, the limit of Albert's pocket money. The other boy, cautious about the transaction, demanded the first instalment up front, but Albert said he wouldn't have his sixpence until Friday evening, which meant he couldn't get his hands on the pistol until the following Monday. The boy agreed to wait, and the bargain was struck. Young Albert would become the proud possessor of this authentic working pistol, an instrument of death that he would cherish for most of his life.

After what was for him an agonisingly long weekend, Albert arrived at school uncharacteristically early on Monday morning and wasted no time in seeking out the other party to the transaction. When he found the boy, he handed over his bright silver sixpence – his entire fortune at the time – not caring that he'd mortgaged away his entire income for the next half-year; that didn't matter. All that mattered was that the pistol should be his.

In a whispered conversation, Albert was told that the gun had been hidden in the school toilets, behind the cistern in the cubicle in which the bargain had been made. He knew he couldn't retrieve it immediately because then he'd have to carry it with him all day and run the risk of being discovered. So, with a tense and eager anticipation, he managed to sit, squirming on his seat, through the agonisingly long lessons until the final bell rang and he could run down into the toilet block. He stood on the seat, reached up and scrabbled behind the cistern for his prize, eventually retrieving the pistol, which he stuffed into the waistband of his trousers, then he pulled his jumper down over the bulge before running to catch the bus home.

When he reached The Grove, Albert realised that he couldn't show off his treasure; he couldn't take it into the house, where his brothers and sisters or, worse, his parents might discover it. So, when he reached the house, he didn't enter via the back door, as usual, his arrival announced by the clattering of his boots on the floor. Instead, he crept silently, like an Indian brave, down to his father's greenhouse, where he carefully hid the pistol behind the flowerpots, which weren't due to be disturbed until the following spring. Then, with a carefree whistle, he went in for his tea.

Just owning the gun, however, wasn't enough for Albert. After all, what use is a gun without bullets? Luckily, his benefactor came to his rescue the next week and told him that he'd discovered in his father's desk drawer a single bullet that he believed would fit the pistol.

After school that day, Albert and his friend went out into the depths of the appropriately named Deadman's Wood, where Albert loaded the round into an empty chamber, closed the pistol, aimed it at a nearby tree and pulled the trigger. Suddenly, there was an ear-splitting explosion and pain flashed up Albert's wrist, almost breaking it. Despite this, he was fiercely proud: he'd fired his first pistol, and he still remembers the event with fondness, recalling, 'My ears were ringing. In fact, they're still ringing now. They haven't stopped ringing since.'

After finally (and thankfully) leaving school in 1955, Albert worked on a farm for two years. Every day he would cycle the twelve miles there and the twelve miles back, come rain, snow or shine. Always a diligent worker, he enjoyed the agricultural life – the animal husbandry, the fresh air, the open spaces and the hulking farm machinery, which he would operate with an unbridled enthusiasm, even taking home broken parts and repairing them and manufacturing new ones on a second-hand engineering lathe. Indeed, by this stage in his life, Albert was consumed with a passionate interest in anything mechanical and had gained an informal rudimentary knowledge of metalworking through trial and error.

As soon as he had the chance of a job at Consett Steelworks, Albert decided to leave working on the land as a career path, although it would remain an interest of his for the rest of his life. Almost as soon as he had arrived at the works, however, he was laid off, as there was insufficient work owing to the volatile nature of the steel industry, which was still largely in private ownership at the time.

After this initial disappointment, Albert joined the Army, but as soon as his basic training was completed he left, under somewhat obscure circumstances. It might reasonably be assumed, however, that his dislike for authority in any form could have been a major factor.

On his return to Consett, Albert found that there was little work available, but he managed to find a job digging ditches for the local council. At least this meant that he was outdoors again, and it gave him plenty of time to pursue his true interests, which lay elsewhere.

By the early 1960s, Albert had acquired something of a local reputation for being able to mend and adapt firearms. People would come to him with obsolete firearms or parts of guns and he would attempt to repair them or cobble together new ones, even making ammunition for them. Rumour had it that, if you lived in the Consett area and wanted to acquire a gun for shooting vermin, Albert Dryden was the man to see. It was highly probable that the component parts of many of these weapons had been liberated from the proceeds of the local constabulary's regular firearms amnesties, which would normally have been burned at Consett Steelworks on a periodic basis. Albert would later claim that most of these manufactured guns were merely replicas designed to hang above the fireplace and had no other use, but he also confessed that he and his friends used to go out and shoot deer to supply their customers with venison, and by his own admission he was 'capable of handling a gun'.

Dryden's claim of having a good safety record with guns is questionable, for he was injured at least twice by stray bullets. The first such accident occurred on an improvised firing range in 1958, when he was accidentally shot in the hand by a .22 rifle.

The second and potentially more lethal accident

34

occurred in 1962, when Dryden was twenty-two, and in almost inconceivable circumstances. Always looking for adventure, Albert was inspired to re-enact the story of William Tell, thinking that there could be nothing like the thrill of shooting at another human being. He and his friends must have had extreme confidence in each other, as they'd been practising shooting tin cans off each other's heads. When it was his turn, Albert paced his way to the tree and turned to grin hugely at his mates, trying not to show his nerves. Then he carefully placed the can on his head, saw his friend squinting over the sights of his Colt revolver, saw his finger tighten on the trigger... and then Albert's whole world exploded in noise, light and pain. He fell to the ground, clutching his head, fearing for a moment that he'd been blinded until he wiped the curtain of blood from his eyes with his sleeve. He still bears a groove in his scalp that tracks the bullet's path.

Having fuelled his interest in firearms with American magazines such as *Guns and Ammo*, it was at about this time that Albert acquired a 9mm Luger pistol, a weapon that was recovered many years later from his house at Priestman Avenue. He remembers one occasion when he was walking over the moorland fells to Egglestone with the gun in his pocket (no doubt looking for some sport for target practice) when two policemen whom he knew came up to him and stopped him. He alleges that he'd taken out the Luger to demonstrate to the officers how it worked, and in his version of events the policemen soon drove off as they realised he knew what he was doing and didn't want to get involved.

It's not clear what actually happened on this occasion, although a retired officer remembers meeting Dryden in that location at about that time, and he also recalls having a fair idea that he was up to no good and that it would most probably involve guns, although he can't recall actually being shown the pistol.

Dryden alleges that it was on this occasion that he shot his first deer, presumably with that same pistol. The souvenirs of that kill – a set of antlers – still exist, screwed on to a wall upstairs in Dryden's old house in Priestman Avenue. The bullet that killed the deer went straight through the animal, then ploughed into a silver-birch tree. Dryden recovered the slug, and it currently resides in a blackened tobacco box by the fireside in the same house, a mute testament to Dryden's 'remarkable marksmanship', or perhaps a tale somehow embellished in the telling.

Without a firearms licence, it was impossible for Dryden to acquire ammunition through lawful channels, so he had to resort to making his own. A loophole in the system (one that's now thankfully closed) allowed him to acquire legally the component parts to do this. His sister, Elsie, remembers, 'Albert used to ask me to go to Bagnall & Kirkwood in Newcastle to get different things. I remember him asking me to go and get sulphur and stuff like that, and him having little pots and making his own bullets for guns.'

As well as ammunition, Albert also manufactured

reloading cartridges for his weapons, moulding the bullets out of lead in his workshop. His favourite weapon was still the first gun he possessed, a Webley, for which he formed heavier than usual bullets that he referred to fondly as 'manstoppers'.

This passion for anything that exploded also strayed into the realm of unmanned flight, and in his workshop Albert planned and constructed rockets that he would set off indiscriminately, with considerable danger to life and limb. Using the expertise he'd gained from making cartridges for his guns, he mixed his own 'rocket fuel' for these larger missiles after having acquired some literature and advice on the subject from a friend named Vic in America who allegedly had other friends who were involved in rocket research at Oklahoma University.

Albert claimed that he had set off his first rocket in October 1958 on the moors above Derwentside. His experiments in this arena reached their apex in 1961 when he enjoyed what should have been his only fifteen minutes of fame, when he and his friends launched a large rocket that narrowly missed a Vulcan bomber flying overhead on a training run over Derwentside and Weardale. As a result of this escapade, Albert appeared in court and was fined the not inconsiderable sum of £180. In characteristically precise form, he would later claim 117 successes at setting off rockets and maintained that he could fire a missile fourteen miles into the air.

In 1966, an opportunity arose for Albert to return to the Consett Steelworks as a storeman, and the following year the works became part of the newly nationalised British Steel Corporation, which afforded (amongst other things) better job security for its employees, enabling Albert to remain in constant employment until 1980, when the works finally closed. His workmates described him as something of a character, an eccentric, and his cowboy interests and antics proved to be a source of amusement and irritation. It wasn't unknown for him, for example, to dress as a cowboy within the works, and he was even seen at times carrying a pistol.

During this time, with money in his pocket from a constant wage, Albert developed another interest: large American cars. He owned a number of US models over the years, acquiring Oldsmobiles, Pontiacs, Cadillacs, a Chrysler and a Lincoln. Amongst these was a 1978 Oldsmobile that he adapted, welding on parts and hammering out new panels to construct what he claimed was the longest car in the world at 27ft 4in long. He would happily tinker with his automobiles from dawn to dusk and was often seen around Consett in one or other of his luxury vehicles. As an early venture into the world of business, he even offered them, with little success, for hire as wedding cars, but, as he lacked sufficient acumen to make the project work, it soon foundered.

Despite his new comfortable financial status, Albert avoided the excesses of an extravagant lifestyle. He didn't smoke, wasn't really interested in darts, drink or women and went to bed early. He claims to have had seventeen relationships since 1956, the longest of which lasted for eight and a half years and ended in July 1988. This was with Margaret Bennett, who was a year younger than Albert and, according to him, asked him to marry her more than fifty times, although he refused on each occasion, not wanting to settle down. Generally, he appears to have been well liked, a quiet lad who had something of a reputation as a fantasist but who could tell a good story, a skill that made him fairly popular. There was, according to one of his contemporaries, 'something about him that people just took to'.

The Drydens' family life was regular and uneventful. Albert's eldest brother, Leslie, emigrated to Australia in 1964, while his eldest sister, Audrey, died tragically in 1972, at the age of forty, following a stroke. Albert's next sister, Elsie, married Peter Donnelly and lived with him in Consett, not far from the family home, while his younger sister, Nora, married and worked as a domestic in a local hospital. Brother George, meanwhile, married and worked as a carpenter, while Ann lived with her family and husband, who was a draughtsman.

Albert was left at home with his mother and brother Alan (who suffered from Down's syndrome and diabetes), both of whom he cared for until they died. Every Sunday morning, as though performing a sacred duty, Albert would go around to his sister Elsie's house for a brief cup of tea with her family, and in the afternoon, as was the habit with extended families in the area, Elsie would reciprocate and take her children around to visit her mother in the afternoon at The Grove, where they would have tea. On these occasions, Albert would always manage to come in late, after which he would eat his tea quietly and then, as soon as politeness allowed, go out to his shed, usually followed by Elsie's children, Simon and Joanna. There the kids would sit on boxes in the corner as Albert worked on his metal lathe and told them tall tales of the Wild West that made their mouths fall open and their eyes stretch as wide as saucers. Uncle Albert was always the best storyteller they'd ever known.

Albert liked a well-regulated, orderly life, and later, after the death of his mother, he described his daily programme: 'I'd get up at eight o'clock and Alan would get up at the same time. He'd see to the fire while I prepared the breakfast. Then we'd clean our teeth and, if it was pension day, I'd get the pension. I'd back the car from the garage and go to Consett and shop. We did our shopping every day. You don't need a fridge in this country; it's not warm enough.'

After spending a day on his smallholding, tinkering with his cars, caring for his animals or planting, he would come home in the early evening, between 4.30pm and 7.00pm. Alan would have a simple cooked meal waiting for him, and the pair would go to bed at around 9.30 each evening, whereupon Albert, while lying in his bed, waiting for sleep to take him, would methodically think over his programme for the next day.

FOUR

Albert Dryden was made redundant from Consett Steelworks in 1980 and was awarded a substantial redundancy payment, which he used to purchase a general dealer's store in nearby Lanchester, intending that his then girlfriend, Margaret Bennett, would run it and that it would provide him with a steady income. Still fascinated by large American cars, he wanted to devote all his time to restoring his beloved 'Yanks'. Not only did he restore the models he bought, but on some he would also make structural changes to make them look even more bizarre. Suffice to say that his hobby or, rather, his obsession for these monsters did not endear him to Margaret, as he would regularly meet her in clothes smudged with oil. After seven or eight months, the store foundered and Albert was forced to sell it, making a profit (according to him) of some £500 on the sale of the premises.

Until this time, Albert had always repaired his own cars at his home in Priestman Avenue and, now that he had more time on his hands, he started working on other people's there, too.

By 1983, always on the lookout for a money-making scheme, Albert decided to diversify and bought a chainsaw with which to cut up logs, which he then sold. Never a shirker by any means, and always industriously pursuing one activity or other, he had little concept of what was socially acceptable in terms of his hours of working, and his endeavours with his chainsaw soon brought him into conflict with his next-door neighbours, who were less than enamoured of the irksome yet productive little man next door.

One of these neighbours was the brother of a General Municipal Boilerworkers' Union official who worked at a senior level in the direct service organisation of Derwentside District Council. There was already some history of enmity between the two, as Albert had already complained, back in 1981, about the noise made by his neighbour's beagles. However, Albert's anti-social activities also sparked off a second complaint, from someone who coincidentally also worked for the local district council, in the local taxation department, again regarding Albert's log-cutting activities and his round-the-clock mechanics.

Because of the noise issue, the council's Environmental Health Department was brought into contact with Albert

Dryden for the first time, an encounter that predictably resulted in a flurry of accusations and counter-accusations between Albert and his neighbours. Councils are well used to such disputes, however, although it's unfortunate that they get caught in the crossfire of such spats, which often degenerate into a tit-for-tat battle between the two sides, after which both parties will more often than not turn on the council. This was certainly the case with Albert, and these incidents served to colour his relationship with the authority from that point onwards.

On this occasion, another department of the council also became involved as, by selling the logs he cut, Albert was using the premises for a commercial purpose. The Planning Department investigated this aspect of the affair and began its fateful dealings with Dryden as, for the first time, it was authorised to take enforcement proceedings against him. In the event, these activities ceased as Dryden began to look for other land in the area.

Following the closure of Consett Steelworks, an act that brought widespread unemployment to the area, in the hopes of economic regeneration Derwentside District Council had begun to reclaim the defunct company's land, which involved the transfer of ownership of parcels of land to the council for not inconsiderable sums. There were certain areas, however, that were of little use to the council themselves and which they proposed to sell off if they were ever acquired. One of these was at the bottom of The Grove, not far from where Albert lived. Once he heard about this, Albert saw the purchase of this land as an answer to all his problems, as he'd be able to continue his log-sawing and car-repairing businesses there and maybe even keep some livestock, which he had always wanted to do.

By this stage, the council were pursuing their enforcement proceedings against Albert, although they were hoping for an informal resolution to the dispute. In the meantime, Albert had submitted another planning application, this one requesting permission to change the store in Lanchester into a car-repair workshop, but this was refused as it was judged that it would cause disturbance to neighbours. This application was dealt with by Harry Collinson himself, and it's likely that the pair first met during these negotiations.

Meanwhile, Albert's feud with his neighbours at Priestman Avenue continued unabated, and on one occasion, as Dryden made one of his many unscheduled visits to the council's offices, he found one of his next-door neighbours – the brother of the union official – in the reception area. Immediately, he assumed that the man had come to make further complaints about him (although this wasn't the case) and, despite the fact that the man was holding a child in his arms, Dryden attacked him without provocation, having to be prised off the man by Planning Department staff.

Not long after this incident, the council's chief housing officer received a visit from Dryden, during which the latter alleged collusion between his victim and members of the council's Environmental Health Department over the proposed purchase of the land at The Grove. On this occasion, the police were not informed.

The situation regarding the site at The Grove had, by now, moved on. Although the council hadn't yet formally purchased the site, Albert had sought to steal a march on any other would-be purchasers by submitting a planning application to use the site for wood-cutting, car-repairing and vegetable-growing. After a considerable saga, this application was eventually refused in early 1984, although a group of council officers – including Harry Collinson – were asked to assist him in finding alternative sites for his proposed business.

Ultimately, the council didn't proceed with their plan to purchase the site at The Grove. Instead, the land was eventually acquired privately by a council employee. No other purchaser could have incited Dryden further, and he was now convinced that there had been some underhand dealing over the sale, which merely served to fuel his already wild suspicions of corruption within the council. This resentment would eventually prompt him to go to the police for the first time, and it hardened his attitudes in his future dealings with Derwentside District Council.

Meanwhile, Margaret Bennett's mother owned a small piece of land at a place called Butsfield, just off the main A68, between Castleside and Tow Low. It's hard to find on any map. On a leafy country road called Eliza Lane, the land in question was a small plot of pasture surrounded by a copse of trees – pretty, but of little significance in planning terms – and boasted a number of agricultural buildings, all derelict. Using all his powers of persuasion, Dryden managed to lease this from Mrs Bennett in 1982, presumably as a place where he could get on with his activities undisturbed.

According to his family, Albert intended eventually to build a summerhouse on his girlfriend's mother's land for the enjoyment of his mother and brother Alan. Indeed, until her death, his mother would visit the plot in the summer, describing it as a very pleasant spot, while the rest of the family felt that, if nothing else, Albert's new project would keep him occupied and out of mischief. He eventually managed to buy the land outright from Mrs Bennett in 1984. Now the proud owner of his own land, Albert took the view that this gave him the right to do with it as he pleased. (It's an interesting irony to note that he used the council's own solicitor, Michael Dunstan, to act for him in the purchase. On this occasion, he was on Albert's side, but that wasn't always to be the case.)

Not long after buying the land, Albert applied for a firearms' certificate, which would enable him to purchase a weapon with which to hunt deer, although just where Albert proposed to do his deerstalking was never made clear. In any case, his application was immediately refused by the Durham Constabulary on a number of grounds, including the curiously worded reason that he wouldn't be permitted to possess it without incurring danger to the public. If that was indeed the case, it would have been logical to have expected a more thorough investigation of his background before the final, tragic stages of the future enforcement proceedings.

A further reason for disallowing his application, meanwhile, was that he'd made a false declaration by omitting to include on his application form mention of his previous criminal conviction, for almost hitting a plane with a home-made rocket. Nevertheless, after a lifetime's interest in guns, the lack of formal permission wasn't sufficient to deter Albert from continuing to pursue his favourite hobby.

At that time, there were already two buildings on the site where Albert intended to restart his woodcutting business: a small horse stable and the Young Butsfield Farmers' Community Hall, which was in something of a dilapidated state and hadn't seen any activity for many years. Albert had a vision, however, and, as the weeks passed, his ideas developed and took on a more substantial, concrete form.

Albert had dreamed up a scheme whereby he would build a shed in which he'd keep calves, and then set up some type of horticultural enterprise on the site. He remembered that he'd met an assistant planner at the council – Harry Collinson, whom he had found to be something of a kindred spirit – and so he visited the council offices to seek him out and ask his advice.

It is plain from the correspondence that took place between Harry and the council's planning officer that Harry was initially prepared to encourage Dryden's desire to establish a smallholding and even went as far as to suggest that he should plant a copse of trees at the frontage of the site and install some other planting around the boundaries. It's probable that Harry advised Dryden on how to carry this out, and possibly even provided him with some of his own saplings that he'd grown from seed. They were to be seen walking the bounds of the plot, frequently stopping to admire some woodland flowers nestled between the tangled roots of the established trees, and, according to Dryden, they had occasionally sat on a bench and sipped the scalding tea that he'd brewed and talked about the future.

When this first, somewhat ramshackle structure was completed, Albert bought himself three calves as the beginning of his farming venture. By 1986, two additional greenhouses had been established on the site (both, according to Dryden, by virtue of verbal permission) along with a caravan, and the two buildings previously on the site had been demolished. Dryden always argued that the works had been carried out with Harry's knowledge and implied consent, and indeed Harry had written to the county council on Albert's behalf to enquire into whether there might be financial assistance available to help with the costs of planting trees to screen the land. In the letter, Harry had apparently been complimentary about the standard of Dryden's work, although the second 'greenhouse' had given some cause for concern, as there didn't appear to be much glass used in its construction. This version of events, including the informal acceptance of the building activities, was never later disputed by the council.

The council's own files reveal that, by February 1988,

Dryden had drawn up plans of a bungalow for the site, although at that stage he still hadn't filed a formal planning application, possibly because Harry had informally advised Dryden that he would be unlikely to get permission for such a building. Dryden was undeterred, however, and, in an extraordinary attempt to circumvent the planning rules, he decided to go ahead and build the bungalow anyway, in a hole in the ground, reasoning that, if the height of the tip of the roof was no more than 6ft above normal ground level, he wouldn't need planning permission. At that stage, the intended use of the building was unclear; it had been described at various times as a retirement bungalow, a summerhouse and even a nuclear-fallout shelter.

In May, Dryden excavated the hole, scattering the earth in large mounds around the site, and by June he was digging the foundations. It seemed that the deeper he dug, the lower his and Harry's relationship plummeted. (Dryden later claimed that council officials had visited the site but had made no objections to his work, although the council had no record of any such visit.) As Dryden placed each course of bricks, the enmity between him and the council grew at a rate equal to that of the bungalow.

By April 1989, the council had received two verbal complaints, from separate sources, about Dryden's activities at East Butsfield. This proved to be the final straw; the situation could be ignored no longer, and Harry Collinson was spurred into decisive action. He and his colleague Jack Chown decided to ask the council members for their agreement to begin enforcement proceedings against Dryden, justifying their proposal upon the building of the bungalow without the benefit of planning permission, the complaints the council had received and their perceived opinion that the site was an eyesore. Dryden was then informed by letter that he should cease building immediately, as the previously lenient attitude of the planning authority towards his work on the land had been transformed by the construction of the bungalow and the situation could no longer be allowed to continue.

Jim Wright, the council's enforcement officer, met with Dryden where he was conducted on a tour of the site and he saw for himself what Dryden was claiming, at that time, to be a nuclear-fallout shelter. Wright was appalled; the structure was considerably more than a bunker, and it resembled an almost completed bungalow, presumably designed for human occupation. It was built in a higgledy-piggledy fashion, part of it in brick and part in breezeblock, with some sections of wall even made of wood. There was a random, haphazard distribution of windows and the roof was only partially tiled, interspersed with bits of rusting corrugated tin and Perspex sheets. It is fair to say that he had never seen anything to compare with the construction, and his breath was taken away by Dryden's sheer effrontery of describing this amateur, dangerous and ramshackle structure as an abode fit for human habitation. He'd seen barns built better, and he wondered if that was what the goats that were comfortably inside thought it should be.

Wright couldn't help wondering how things had got to such a pitch and whether Harry's initial appreciation and unwitting support for such an apparently downtrodden individual had been responsible for getting the council into this position in the first place. He felt that, if the matter had been dealt with by someone more straight down the line, such as Jack Chown, Dryden would have never got so far with his absurd project.

Dryden, in his usual pedantic manner, informed Wright that his solicitor had told him that buildings under 59in above ground level didn't require planning permission. However, what exactly was ground level was to prove a contentious point, as Dryden would contend that it should be measured from where the surface had been before his excavations took place. (In reality, even using this yardstick, the building was 4in too high.) The authority, however, took the view that ground level began at the level of the building's foundations.

Jim Wright suggested that Dryden should discuss the matter with Harry Collinson, and Dryden immediately hurried down to the council offices, where he was shown into Harry's office, whereupon the door was firmly shut. There is no record of what was said in the room, although after a few moments the sound of raised voices and intemperate language could be heard by those in adjoining offices.

Soon afterwards, the door flew open and Dryden stormed out. Within just a few days, a set of rudimentary plans for the bungalow arrived on Collinson's desk.

FIVE

Derwentside District Council's Development Subcommittee convened on 9 May 1989 and formally decided to commence enforcement proceedings against Albert Dryden. An enforcement notice was subsequently issued by the Planning Department that was scheduled to come into effect on 26 June and ordered the demolition of all the buildings on the site within three months. As a part of the quasi-legal process associated with this notice, the council was required to give Dryden an official booklet that outlined his rights to appeal against it and how he could go about it. And so on 14 June Albert Dryden appealed to the Department of the Environment against Derwentside District Council's decision, whereupon letters began to fly thick and fast, with Dryden writing to his Member of Parliament, Hilary Armstrong, and anyone else who he thought might be able to bring influence to bear.

It was at this point that events began to take an ominous turn and Dryden started making threats against council officials. 'Well, they can all watch out,' he once warned Jim Wright at Derwentside Civic Centre in Consett. 'I'll start from the top down to you. I know where Peter Hunter [chief environmental services officer and Harry Collinson's ultimate boss] lives and his car number. He'll be first, and then Harry Collinson, right down the line. The dark nights are coming in now and, if Peter Hunter comes to work one morning with a smashed windscreen because a brick has gone through it, you'll know why.'

Then, in September, a telephone call was made to Peter Hunter's home, received by his son, purportedly from a Mr Kelly, who promised that Peter would be 'kneecapped' and perhaps sent to Mounsett Crematorium if Dryden wasn't left in peace. This time the threats were serious enough to report to the police.

In fact, it had become commonplace for Dryden to issue threats of violence when he visited the Civic Centre, many of which were recorded by Mike Bonser, the head of administration there. The frequency of Dryden's threats fostered a sense of complacency amongst the staff, who became so familiar with his rhetoric that they passed it off as the idle chat of a dissatisfied but somewhat eccentric resident.

Harry Collinson was one of the few council employees who was still prepared to listen to Dryden, and he tried on numerous occasions to reason with the disgruntled landowner and explain, in general terms, the relevant planning procedures involved in building a structure like the 'bungalow', but even he was unable to beat a path through Dryden's blind prejudice. Harry's calm reasoning frustrated Dryden, who would often become agitated and, on at least one occasion, claimed that he'd mined the site at Eliza Lane and promised that anyone who dared to venture there would 'have their legs blown off'. Understandably, this attitude was not calculated to further his case.

Then, on Friday, 13 February – an inauspicious date – there was a planning inquiry, which was remembered by some as an absolute farce, although records show that it was properly conducted in all respects. Dryden had co-opted the assistance of his brother-in-law, Peter Donnelly, who had helped him to put together a coherent written argument in favour of his appeal with which to represent him on that day. Donnelly was an articulate man, if a little bombastic, who saw some validity in Dryden's claims and sought to help the smaller man to the best of his ability. He had qualified as a secondary-school teacher late in life and understood the need for some attempt at logical argument in these circumstances.

On the day of the inquiry, the Department of the Environment's inspector presided over what was to become something of a bear-garden. Harry was absent, as was usual in these kinds of circumstances, leaving the matter to Jack Chown. Collinson's absence further infuriated Dryden, who began to lose what little composure he had.

Meanwhile, in the press seats was Mark Summers, a reporter with the *Northern Echo* working at Stanley, who had taken an interest in the case and was covering the appeal inquiry, which he thought might be a novelty item for his readership, bearing in mind the main protagonists – and he was proved right. These were usually arcane, tedious and incomprehensible affairs, not usually the stuff to sell newspapers, but when Dryden took centre-stage the whole proceedings lit up, becoming diverting and almost verging on the ridiculous. Summers later recalled that he and his colleagues were trying their best to suppress their laughter throughout the proceedings. Dryden kept on referring to the planning inspector as 'the Minister' and continued to make personal attacks upon the members and officers of the council, accusing them of falsehood, prevarication and corruption. He threatened that, if he didn't get his way, he would be quite prepared to sell the land, out of spite, to some gypsies, whom he referred to as 'Big Red' and 'Rhona', who have never been identified to this day but who would doubtless take over the site as an encampment.

The inspector wasn't required to hand down his decision that day, which was fortunate because, had he done so, he might well have sparked off a riot. Instead, he took away with him all the submissions from both sides and, after a period of earnest consideration, gave his conclusions. In his letter dated 7 March 1990, he ruled that the bungalow would have to come down, together with the second greenhouse. The other two buildings would escape this fate, as he deemed that they had been constructed outside the time frame that was required for the commencement of enforcement proceedings.

Dryden immediately rushed into print, writing, 'There is no way that this is the end of it. I want to appeal to the High Court in London, and if I lose there I'll go all the way to Europe. If the council tries to come here and knock it down, they will have to do it over my dead body.'

In fact, no appeal against the Inspector's decision was ever lodged at the High Court. While Dryden at first seemed to have a grasp of events around him, this appeared to diminish considerably over time and his perception of the appeal's outcome was certainly noticeably different from that of the council. He was always willing to talk to the press, but it was at about this time that reason and sense seemed to disappear completely from his rants. His conflicts with council officials had become more commonplace, and from being viewed, at best, as an eccentric, he was now seen as a crackpot. According to his brother-in-law, the reality was that he was sinking into an abyss of despair, without support or hope.

Dryden made little effort to comply with the enforcement notice and demolish the buildings, and he began to complain vociferously about visits by council officers, which he felt was tantamount to spying on him. He reiterated his warnings of there being explosives buried on the site, and he became so paranoid that he took to sleeping in his caravan.

In November 1990, Dryden was stirred to resurrect the matter of the piece of land at The Grove that he'd originally intended to purchase, after discovering that the land had been sold to a council employee. It was Dryden's understanding that it was the employee's intention to obtain the necessary planning permission for the construction of housing, and then to resell the land at a massive profit. Incensed at what he saw as gross deception against him, he made a formal complaint to Durham Police, alleging corrupt practice by the district council. His allegations were comprehensively investigated by the police, who found that not only was there no evidence for corruption but also that the land had never actually been bought by the district council from British Steel.

By this time, the relationship between Harry and Albert had worn thin, almost to the extent of open antagonism whenever they met. This was certainly true of Albert, who had gathered around him a coterie of friends and hangers-on, all of whom seemed to want to be involved with Albert's showdown with officialdom. Some of his cronies even took to ringing Collinson on his behalf, such as a man named John Graham, who called the planning officer on 24 January 1991 and ranted and raved at Harry for several minutes, during which time he confirmed that Dryden wasn't prepared to demolish the bungalow and that they, Dryden's friends, would be taking out a summons against Harry Collinson for trespass. Mr Graham apparently said that Dryden was a fighting man and that there was going to be trouble.

Then, on 7 March 1991, Graham himself came to the offices of Derwentside District Council carrying a live cockerel under his arm and demanding to see Peter Hunter, who wasn't in fact available. Hearing of this visit, however, Harry Collinson came down to speak to him. Graham became agitated and would brook no discussion with Harry, and then hurled the cockerel at him in a scene that can barely be imagined. The bird was finally recaptured, and Hunter did eventually consent to see Graham. Nonetheless, the incident left Harry shaken, and the beginnings of a real disquiet about this saga were dawning upon him.

At 4.00pm on 25 March 1991, Harry Collinson and Jim Wright visited Dryden's smallholding at Butsfield. Collinson learned that Dryden had told Wright never to go on to his land again unannounced. Instead, if the enforcement officer wished to contact Dryden, he should sit in his car on the edge of the property and sound his car horn. However, this didn't suit Harry's purpose, which was to serve a summons upon Dryden for a court appearance on 17 April 1991, so he parked out of sight of Dryden's land and the two men got out of the car and walked up to the site.

The gate to the site was open and Harry went in first, followed by Wright. Dryden was standing near his bungalow as they approached. Harry walked up to him and informed him that it was his intention to take some photographs. Dryden refused his permission, so Harry took out the envelope containing the summons and put it in the top pocket of Dryden's overalls. Dryden took out the envelope and regarded it suspiciously and then told Harry and Wright to leave the site, saying as they did so that they had never had his permission to enter the land.

In fact, both men had written authority to enter Dryden's property for the purposes of ensuring compliance with the Planning Acts, but there seemed little point in provoking yet another confrontation, so the two men moved to an adjacent field, intending to photograph Dryden's site from there.

Dryden then came over and approached Wright. An argument ensued, and Dryden began to chase the enforcement officer across the field. Collinson ran towards them and found them both getting up from the ground as he reached them. It appeared that Dryden had struck Wright.

Dryden then began to make wild threats concerning the use of firearms against Harry Collinson and said that he would 'come to his house', warning him that the door wouldn't stop him. He also issued a threat again the Planning Committee, shouting at Wright, 'The next person to go up to Butsfield from the council will have his brains blown out.'

Collinson and Wright walked back to their car, both severely shaken. During Wright's tussle with Dryden, the enforcement officer had lost his watch and his glasses, so they went straight to Consett Police Station to file a complaint against Dryden. They noted their grievances to a young constable named Steven Campbell, who was to figure later in events. At his request, Harry returned to his office and wrote a detailed statement, including some typewritten notes detailing all of the verbal threats Dryden had made against him, as well as the chilling gesture he'd made by putting two fingers together like a gun and placing them under Harry's chin, saying as he did so, 'The next time you come up here, there'll be a bullet here.' After some consultation with his immediate superiors, Campbell advised that, on the next occasion the council's officers were required to serve a summons on Dryden, it would be prudent to arrange for them to be accompanied by a police officer.

PC Campbell later arranged for Dryden and his solicitor to visit the police station, where the would-be farmer was formally interviewed regarding the matter. Campbell quickly gained the impression that Dryden obviously felt victimised but appeared to be very sure of his facts as well as intelligent, despite his oily, dirty, bearded appearance. At the conclusion of the interview (in which Dryden's version of events predictably varied greatly from the council officers'), there was little conclusive evidence to support a charge; it was Collinson and Wright's word against Dryden's.

It is remarkable that, despite the references in the council officers' statements to the possibility of Dryden possessing firearms, no further investigation was made. The file was returned to PC Campbell, inscribed with the words, 'No further action.'

Harry later decided to go back to Dryden's site on his own in order to retrieve Wright's spectacles. After a brief search, he found them in the field where the struggle had taken place.

The next day, Dryden rang Harry and told him that he'd found Wright's glasses, telling them that he'd leave them on the boundary wall of the property for Harry to collect. During the conversation, Harry hadn't mentioned his visit the previous day and, once he'd put down the telephone, he immediately telephoned Consett Police Station. He was severely rattled, believing that Dryden was trying to lure him to Butsfield. The WPC who took his call advised him against returning.

Harry then discussed his suspicions with his colleague Mike Bonser, who then rang the police again, speaking first to an inspector and then to the local commander, Superintendent Hegarty, asking them directly to intervene in the dispute before someone was hurt. This wasn't the first time Bonser had called to express his concern for the safety of his employees in the light of Dryden's behaviour. The only response he got, though, was: 'Don't worry.' The apparent lack of concern at this stage would come back to haunt the police at a later date.

It was obvious that the confrontation that he and Jim Wright had with Dryden had a profound effect upon Harry Collinson, who was, after all, an avowed pacifist. He composed a memo that was circulated to all the staff of the district council, bearing the header 'Albert Dryden' and a photo taken from a local newspaper article, and which advised staff about the potential for violence that Dryden had exhibited towards council employees. The memo was designed to put his colleagues on their guard, should Dryden re-enter the council's offices, and it exhorted them to contact the police should there be suspicion of a physical confrontation with the man.

Certainly, by this stage, no one could accuse the council of being complacent about Dryden. His latest behaviour added fuel to the rumours about him and his penchant for firearms that were buzzing around the offices and the town. Even Harry's girlfriend, Caroline Mason, got to hear the gossip and tackled him about it, expressing her concern for his safety. He reportedly advised her, 'Don't answer the door if you're worried about that.'

At this time, Dryden was telephoning the council offices every day, delivering accusations that were becoming more and more lurid and extravagant. He was frustrated by an apparent lack of response from the council, when in truth there was little left to say. Finally, on 11 June 1991, the council's solicitor, Michael Dunstan, wrote to Dryden at his home to the effect that, in accordance with their instruction, the council's contractors would be carrying out the removal operation on 20 June 1991.

Dryden, however, was undeterred, and the level of his threats intensified. Typically, he told reporter Mark Summers that he would load up the Yank (one of his extended American cars) with explosives and drive it into the Civic Centre to 'blow the lot to Kingdom come'.

The last thing Harry Collinson said to his family about

the situation at Butsfield, on the occasion of his niece's wedding, on the Saturday preceding the proposed demolition, was: 'It's ridiculous. I don't know what the man is thinking. The water drains into it. You just couldn't live like that; it's impossible. The whole thing is just so ridiculous.'

And so it was.

SIX

Along with the usual run of dreary council planning business, distinct from inspecting drains and discussing whether a new house could have mock–Tudor beams, Derwentside District Council was actually contemplating knocking down a building. This was a notable occurrence, an uncommon event, and the circumstances required those involved to consider carefully how it would be achieved.

The significant factor in this situation was the person that they were dealing with. Everyone on the council knew of Albert Dryden and had heard of his now-infamous assault with a deadly cockerel. He was known to be rash and volatile, with a propensity to threaten violence and an innate distrust of authority in any form. It was also now clear that he could only too easily be forced into crossing the line into violent retaliation.

Over the years, Dryden had made bellicose threats against council officers and others who had crossed him. He was well known for being irrational, and those on the council couldn't discount him as simply another irate landowner who would mutter while his pride and joy was demolished. He had already been reported to the police for offences of assault and criminal damage against council officials over the previous few weeks, and there were ample written records of conversations with Dryden in which he'd threatened to 'burn' some council officials, in his own version of gangster slang. As well as threatening murder, he had made other menaces towards individuals and even threatened that he would blow up the council's offices.

The trouble was that Dryden had made so many threats like this over the years that people on the council often refused to take him seriously, and his reputation as a harmless eccentric often overshadowed the more sinister aspect of his personality.

Harry Collinson was under no such illusions. From his previous relationship with Dryden, where he'd initially felt some empathy with him and managed to rub along with him, two seemingly difficult characters together, Harry had come to the conclusion that there could be no further reasoning with him. He was at a stand-off with no room left for manoeuvre. Ultimately, Harry was a professional planner with certain duties to discharge, and he knew that, whatever personal feelings he might have about Dryden, the bungalow's scheduled demolition would have to go ahead. Although he'd become increasingly aware of Dryden's apparent potential for violence, Harry weighed the pros against the cons and believed that, if he was there to oversee the exercise, then Dryden would listen to him and trust him.

Harry knew that there was no way the council could back down; they'd come this far, exhausted all the possibilities, and it was time for the final curtain. Harry being Harry, however, when discussing the arrangements with Mike Bonser, he was overwhelmingly concerned that everything should be done up front and above board so that the council could be seen to be acting openly and with no collusion. After all, he'd done nothing wrong, and the council had done nothing wrong, so why should the demolition be carried out in secret?

As a town planner, Harry was always on the front line, with everything he did being subject to criticism and detailed examination. He'd lost count of the number of times he'd been humiliated by ignorant councillors in committees or been accused of being corrupt for recommending approval of some controversial planning application or other. Dryden had already alerted the press to his own plight, and some papers had even carried articles about the proposed demolition, most of them coming from the angle of the little man being ground down by a faceless bureaucracy – typical red-top reactionary headlines on which the tabloids thrive.

Why then, reasoned Collinson, should the council not take advantage of this situation and actively encourage the media to be there, to witness for themselves that the council had nothing to hide and was only doing what it was required, by law, to do? Furthermore, if all the press were there – and Harry would do an efficient job of ensuring that they were, including journalists for TV, radio and as many newspapers as he could muster – it would be unlikely that Dryden would cause any trouble.

Bonser, meanwhile, was far more cautious, inclined to opt for a more low-profile approach with as little press involvement as possible. He even suggested that, should any members of the press enquire about when the demolition would be occurring, they should give them the date after the demolition had taken place, after which they could plead that they'd been the victims of an 'administrative error'. This would be easier for the council to handle, he argued, and warned Harry that, if they miscalculated, the whole episode might become Dryden's version of Custer's Last Stand and that he might, true to his word, blow up the buildings.

Harry dismissed Bonser's worries and restated his view that Dryden was all bluster, and that the idea of blowing up the buildings was sheer bravado on his part, yet another product of his overactive imagination. He always gave Dryden the benefit of the doubt and would often defend him like this, perhaps even secretly sympathising with him. When the final tally was counted, however, he was committed to his duty and did what he had to, no matter how much he disliked doing it.

Mike Bonser had a good relationship with the local

police and he pushed Harry in their direction, hoping that they might make him see sense. After all, if the press and Dryden's hangers-on were going to turn the affair into a media circus, it would be appropriate to keep the police informed, if only to ensure that the peace was kept.

In view of these concerns, a meeting was arranged to take place on the Tuesday evening before the demolition at Consett Police Station at Parliament Street, a short walk from the council's offices at Medomsley Road. Ostensibly organised at the request of Derwentside District Council, the meeting was more a personal favour called in by Bonser who, in the meantime, had got Michael Dunstan, the council's solicitor, on his side and with whose help he had convinced Harry to involve the police. Harry was reluctant to contact the authorities, but Bonser and Dunstan wanted to make sure that the police were aware of the circumstances of the dispute and of the council's obligation to take action in respect of the demolition of Dryden's bungalow. They were also acutely aware of the potential for trouble and were keen to have a substantial police presence.

The meeting was attended by Harry, Michael Dunstan, local police Superintendent Stan Hegarty and two of his officers. Also there to add a practical dimension to the discussions were the council officers who would be responsible for clearing out any animals or property from the building before the demolition contractor – who was also present – knocked down the bungalow.

As the meeting began, all groups assembled discussed the

background to the situation and the arrangements for the demolition, which was scheduled to take place that Thursday, only two days away. Harry outlined the current circumstances and the events that had brought them together, emphasising that there was no alternative to demolition. He then gave specific instructions to the demolition contractor about which buildings were to be removed, adamant that the buildings should be completely flattened so that there was no chance of them being reconstructed by Dryden. Meanwhile, nothing was to be taken from the site and any extraneous damage was to be kept to a minimum. He then pointed out that there would be personnel from the council's Direct Service Organisation on site in case there was need to remove any valuables from the buildings prior to their demolition, and that they would be equipped with boltcroppers in case it was necessary to force an entry. No one was to touch Dryden, whatever the provocation, said Harry, and he'd arranged for a video of events to be shot so that there could be no later disputes about what had taken place. He then finished by stating that he'd already contacted the media and that he expected them to be there in force.

It's fair to say that the police don't enjoy getting caught up in what they consider to be civil law situations. They don't consider them to be their primary responsibility and, besides, too often the lines get blurred and things turn messy. It's one thing to maintain a presence during a spat between neighbours over the height of a fence, but the dispute between the council and Albert Dryden was moving up several levels. It couldn't be noted in the station's occurrence book as 'Civil dispute – parties advised'; here they were supporting a local authority in the exercise of their lawful powers, and the local constabulary displayed a marked reluctance to overextend their area of responsibility.

When the time came to discuss the role of the police in the operation, it was decided that they would have two distinct responsibilities. Firstly, they would control the flow of traffic from the main trunk road, the A68, where parking was not permitted, to where it joined Eliza Lane, which was essentially a country lane just wide enough for two vehicles to pass. Bearing in mind that on Thursday morning there would be a gigantic low-loader carrying the bulldozer that would be used to tear down the bungalow, it was going to be a tight fit to get the council officials' cars and police vehicles on to the site, let alone any press that might also decide to turn up. Secondly, the police would maintain law and order during the operation and take appropriate action in the event of any breach of the peace.

This was the bit that always made the police wince. What do you plan for? Where's the fine line between heavy-handed policing and letting things get out of hand? Too many distressing public-order lessons had been learned during the miners' strike of 1984, and police commanders were constantly under pressure to err on the side of caution and not to overstate the police presence. Superintendent Hegarty took pains at the meeting to emphasise that the actual operation was nothing to do with the police, and they would take action only if there was an overt breach of the peace.

However, nobody really addressed the problem of how to deal with the protagonist, Albert Dryden. Hegarty did point out that it might be better for all concerned if the demolition work was carried out at a time when it could be guaranteed that Dryden wasn't on the premises – for example, when he was due to appear in court for the alleged assault on Jim Wright – but this jarred with Harry Collinson, whose honourable principles made him feel that the matter should be brought to a conclusion in an honest and open way, with Dryden present and aware of all the circumstances. To do otherwise, he argued, would leave the way open for Dryden to accuse both the council and the police of acting in an underhand way, which could tarnish their public profiles.

According to those who served under him, Stan Hegarty was a good 'guvnor', a softly spoken, slow-to-anger man with a creased, careworn face tinged from years of smoking. He listened to his men and had never lost touch, as some police commanders are wont to do, being prepared to take advantage of any advice and weigh things up with a big helping of common sense. As he heard the council officers laying out their plans, it seemed that he understood their united concerns about Dryden and the extensive history of threats he'd made against them and their colleagues. During the conversation, mention was made of Dryden's consuming interest in firearms, but the consensus view seemed to be that it was unlikely that he would be reckless enough to do anything violent with the television cameras on him; certainly that was the line that Harry was pushing.

Local knowledge is a necessary tool of the police officer, especially in a rural force, and in this case there was an excessive amount concerning Dryden, who had been the stuff of rumour and gossip for at least thirty years, never venturing far from his home territory. What information-gathering had gone on prior to the meeting can only be the subject of speculation, although amongst the police rank and file there were those who would later say that no one had seen fit to talk to the officers on the ground who had come into contact with Albert Dryden on a day-to-day basis or had known him for some time. Indeed, it later transpired that Dryden was well known to many time-served officers, some of whom would have expressed grave reservations about the plan, had their opinion been sought. It seems entirely likely that those planning the operation were oblivious to the intelligence available to them.

Police officers weren't the only source of intelligence, however. In the months running up to the demolition, a number of reporters had sought to build a rapport with Dryden, including Garry Willey, a reporter with the local *Evening Chronicle*, who had covered the bungalow saga for more than two years. In one piece (later quoted extensively), he made a chilling observation about the circumstances surrounding a conversation he'd allegedly

held with Dryden on the previous Friday, when he'd
visited him at Eliza Lane. On that occasion, he'd heard
Dryden threaten to use firearms to keep Mr Collinson and
any bulldozer crews off his land. 'Albert told me that he
would burn Harry Collinson if he tried to go through
with the demolition,' Willey reported, 'and that he had a
machine gun which he had been practising with on the
moors at Stanhope.' Willey claimed that Dryden had also
shown him a brass cartridge casing to which he had
pointed and bragged that he had some ammunition that
was 'sufficient to cut any JCB in half'. Aghast, Willey had
listened intently as Dryden calmly revealed that he was
prepared to use firepower to defend his bungalow, then
proceeded to lay out the essence of his plan.

When Willey returned to his office, he discussed this
information with an incredulous editor, and between
them, to their credit, the pair decided not to include this
information in the following day's article but to pass it on
immediately to the police. Despite its potential as the
newsprint equivalent of gold dust, they had the sense to
realise that they were in possession of information that
could hold the power of life and death. Instead, Willey
telephoned Consett Police Station and spoke to the duty
inspector, passing on word for word the details of his
conversation with Dryden. (To his eternal chagrin, Willey
never thought to ask the inspector's name, and his
respondent was never later identified, although at that time
there were only three inspectors stationed at Consett Police
Station.) This information was certainly never brought to

the meeting that Tuesday evening and was later dismissed by the police as possibly a merely casual and inconclusive conversation, if indeed it had taken place at all.

Indeed, it was unusual, to say the least, that there was no written record of the exchange at Consett Police Station, especially bearing in mind the fastidiousness of the police when it comes to the accuracy of their record-keeping. No one ever went as far as to suggest that Willey had made the whole thing up. After all, why should he, when he could have easily persuaded his editor to run the piece as a scoop? Of course, even if his information had been available that Tuesday night, it's questionable whether it would have influenced the police's preparations.

On the basis of his discussions with the council officials, Stan Hegarty felt that he had enough information to enable him to draw up an operational order setting out in detail the game plan for dealing with Albert Dryden that Thursday. The order was later signed by Inspector Geoff Young, who was designated to be the officer in charge of the action, and he circulated copies to all those involved. As well as Young – a tried and trusted supervisor – Hegarty allocated two of his own sergeants and four constables and had managed to beg, borrow or steal a few more men from a neighbouring subdivision. These last were put on standby at Consett Police Station, along with a dog handler, a paramedic and a uniformed traffic car that just happened to be one of the force's two ARVs (armed-response vehicles). The briefing was set to take place at Consett Police Station at 0815 hours on Thursday, 20 June 1991.

As the senior executive officer, Assistant Chief Constable Eddie Marchant was responsible for the supervision of potentially difficult police operations, and as such the Butsfield proposal fell within his remit. He recalled later that he was aware of the proposed demolition but is adamant that, to the best of his recollection, there had been no suggestion of firearms in connection with the Dryden operation. There was, apparently, 'insufficient intelligence' to support a police firearms operation, but if there had been then the whole complexion of the planning would have changed, requiring the presence of police negotiators and firearms experts.

The divisional commander at the time, Brian Mackenzie, who was subsequently elevated to the peerage and now sits out his retirement in the House of Lords, only dimly recalls the planning phase of the operation, which he'd left to Hegarty, his subordinate, and was certainly unaware of any potential for the use of weapons. Indeed, his clearest memory about the operation is of reading about it in a newspaper while on holiday in the Canary Islands.

SEVEN

That Thursday, not quite the longest day of the year, the weather looked as though it would be lovely: blue skies with just a hint of wispy cloud and a light, warm breeze. Those policemen on 'early days' – six in the morning until two in the afternoon – were already on the move. This shift was much hated by those selected to work it, as it meant having to 'parade on' at the police station a quarter of an hour before the shift began, which in turn meant getting up at about five o'clock. Small wonder, then, that no one liked early days; you never quite managed to get enough sleep and felt permanently tired all day.

For some of the officers getting up that day, however, their lives would change irrevocably before the sun went down. Events around Consett would ensure that that day would be forever burned into local memory.

On the road by this time were Phil Brown and Andy Reay, the crew of the ARV, call sign Mike 34 Papa. They got on well, understood each other and made a good team, having enjoyed an easy and longstanding relationship. Both were quiet, undemonstrative and softly spoken men. Phil was slight of build with a delicate moustache and was dwarfed by his partner, the bigger, blond Andy. They had both started out as traffic men and had undergone training to drive fast and powerful cars. Besides that, they'd put themselves forward for firearms training and had proved themselves as reliable and competent marksmen. For that day, Phil had been elevated to acting sergeant, a role he had fulfilled many times before, but there wasn't a great deal of supervising to do at six o'clock in the morning.

A couple of years earlier, the Durham Constabulary had decided to follow the national trend and formed an armed-response unit, consisting of two double-crewed cars able to respond to spontaneous firearms incidents. These two units – one patrolling the northern and one the southern divisions of County Durham – would provide twenty-four-hour cover.

Phil and Andy were two of the first in the UK to be trained as armed-response officers, although until that Thursday not a great deal had been required of them, as firearms incidents were, thankfully, still extremely rare.

Every policeman knows that firearms in the police service is a mug's game. It's fine doing the training and playing cowboys and Indians, of course; where else could you get to shoot hundreds of rounds of live ammunition every year? It's most schoolboys' dream, and would certainly have been enough to make Dryden drool at the prospect, but the plain truth is that, as every qualified firearms officer knows, no matter what support he's promised from his superiors or what his friends and colleagues might say, as soon as he pulls that trigger, he suddenly becomes the loneliest man on the planet. His companions drift away from him as if he's a bad smell, not wanting to be tainted by what comes next.

Phil and Andy had both had the probable consequences of discharging a firearm drummed into them by their instructors: the inquiry, the suspicion that they were gung-ho or negligent and being forever associated with a single incident. And if, heaven forbid, they should hit anyone or, even worse, kill them, those consequences would be ten times worse. Nevertheless, there are still a few constables prepared to go through the rigorous training necessary and come out the other side to gain the dubious honour of becoming an authorised firearms officer.

That Thursday, the boot of the 2.5l Vauxhall police car Phil and Andy were driving contained a steel box in which were locked the tools of their trade, including two six-round Smith & Wesson .357 Magnum police service revolvers, which packed an enormous punch and shot to fame as Clint Eastwood's weapon of choice in his *Dirty Harry* movies. Each pistol was equipped with eighteen rounds of semi-jacketed, semi-wadcutter ammunition, each round a flat-nosed bullet designed to dump all its energy into the target and cause maximum damage.

There was also one eight-shot, twelve-bore Remington pump-action shotgun, a devastating weapon in its own right and capable of enormous firepower. Privately owned shotguns of this type had recently been limited to having a maximum capacity of three rounds, and owners of such weapons didn't have access to the more powerful ammunition available to the police.

Both Phil and Andy had been trained extensively with these weapons and were very comfortable with them.

The mobile phone in their car trilled and Phil picked it up.

'Hello, Mike thirty-four Papa.'

'Hi, Phil. It's Dave Blackie.'

I was one of the force's four firearms instructors and tactical advisers, having qualified as a firearms officer eight years earlier and, in 1989, having become an instructor in the police's Support Services Department, which was responsible not only for firearms but also for public order, bomb searches and just about every other hands-on discipline that nobody else wanted to touch. The department trained all of the men it took on – not just the authorised officers but their senior officers as well – and it was also their responsibility, as tactical advisers, to run live firearms incidents, as they understood the routines far better than anyone else.

As part of my duties, I was also involved with training middle-managers, and I was in the office early that day to finalise the arrangements for a firearms exercise designed to demonstrate the abilities under extreme pressure of newly promoted inspectors, checking the day's arrangements to ensure that everything would run smoothly. The scenario was to be a bungled armed robbery at an old warehouse complex, and I'd secured the help of various other departments in putting together an all-singing, all-dancing exercise that would severely test the competence of the inspectors, who had complete control over proceedings. The support staff included negotiators, a specialist tactical firearms team, the press office to badger the candidates with questions, senior officers demanding information updates, hostages, the 'criminals' (who had a brief to be as awkward as possible) and, of course, Phil and Andy, who were to be the first armed officers to be called in.

Along with myself, two other instructors were assisting in ensuring that things ran (or, preferably, didn't run) smoothly that day: John Taylor and Bob Gadd. Both were extremely experienced officers and seemed to have been around firearms in Durham forever.

'Just calling to check that you're still OK for the exercise today,' I said.

Phil replied, 'No, I don't think we can do it. Something's come up.'

'Oh? What?'

'We have to go over to Consett to pick up some ammunition from some old farmer or something,' Phil grumbled. Although briefed, it was apparent that the crew of Mike 34 Papa had little or no idea what was going on. Disappointed at seeing my well-laid plans turned upside down, I said, 'All right, then. I'll count you out of the exercise.'

As I put the phone down, I felt a tingle of unease at the back of my mind. The role of the ARV was to respond to spontaneous firearms incidents, not to go around the county, collecting ammunition at anyone's beck and call. While the officers manning such a vehicle were competent in the use of their weapons, that was really the extent of their training and knowledge. Besides, it was unlikely that they had the necessary expertise to recognise some of the more weird and wonderful weapons and ammunition that the police often encounter. Usually, it was either myself or one of my colleagues who were asked to perform such tasks. And why it had to be done straight away was unfathomable.

At this stage, none of us knew anything of the old farmer to whom Phil had referred, or of Albert Dryden, with whom they would become intimately acquainted in the very near future.

Annoyed at what I believed at the time to be the squandering of valuable resources, I put the thought out of my mind, resolving to speak to the person responsible later in the day, and returned to the preparation of the morning's work.

When they got to Consett Police Station for the 8.15 briefing, Andy and Phil went to the bar (really the only room large enough for such a purpose), squeezing through the door and into a room that was already quite full of uniformed officers, some whom they recognised from Durham subdivision, as well as a dog man and, lo and behold, a paramedic!

A paramedic? What on earth did they want him for? This was turning out to be quite a different kettle of fish to what had been implied by the brief, handwritten note that had been left in Phil's pigeonhole the previous day.

As they entered the bar, copies of what appeared to be an operational order were being handed out, so Andy reached over and grabbed a copy. As they read through it, the two men wondered why they were included in the operation, as it seemed to have little to do with them, and according to the order they weren't even required to leave the police station.

The content was sketchy to say the least, merely saying that, 'DRYDEN is an unpredictable character who has made numerous threats in the past. He was recently arrested for criminal damage and an assault on the council enforcement officer. It is anticipated that DRYDEN will have up to three friends present on the site. Local press and television are aware of the situation and will be in attendance at the scene.'

The general hubbub of conversation subsided as the subdivisional commander, Superintendent Stan Hegarty, and Inspector Geoff Young walked into the room. Stan thanked everyone for coming and then explained that the police had been called into this operation only to help the representatives of the local authority, who were intending to knock down a building that had been built without planning permission. The main purpose of a police presence was to ensure that no breach of the peace took place. Hegarty described Albert Dryden as an eccentric character who might put up a bit of a fight, but stated that he didn't really anticipate any trouble as the council were prepared to back off at any sign of resistance. However, there was a possibility that some of Dryden's friends might be there causing a nuisance, and Hegarty took pains to point out that it was highly likely that some members of the press might also be present and cautioned everyone present to take particular care not to end up in the next day's newspapers for the wrong reasons. Much to Andy and Phil's surprise, there was no mention of firearms being involved; when they asked why they had been included in the operation, they were told that they were there 'to stand by just in case the wheel comes off'.

One of the other Consett officers present at the briefing was young probationer Steven Campbell, who felt a stirring of disquiet at what he heard that day. He recognised Phil and Andy, and he too wondered why they needed an ARV. And why the paramedic? Were they expecting someone to be injured? And what, exactly, did they mean by 'in case the wheel comes off'? Campbell wasn't the only one in that briefing with such questions, but he assumed that, as he hadn't been in the job that long and had never been on a proper operation, this was the way things always were, so he shrugged off his concerns, trusting that his senior officers knew what they were doing.

Just before the briefing broke up, Stan Hegarty opened the floor to questions. Whatever their private thoughts might have been, no one spoke up, perhaps not wanting to look stupid or challenge a senior officer. As they dispersed, the officers switched their radios to the local frequency, channel thirty, and the communications office was deluged with test calls.

All the local officers went downstairs to find transportation to Eliza Lane while the Durham lads and the dog handler sat down in the bar, watching TV. Before long, someone produced a pack of cards. (This aroused a bit of interest. Policemen are accustomed to long waits, standing by to stand by, and any way of passing the time is welcome, especially if it comes with the potential to make a profit.)

Meanwhile, the paramedic, Mike Leonard, stood in a corner, rather alone and forlorn on unfamiliar territory. He'd been detailed to come along by his director of operations at Durham, who'd told him that the Consett Constabulary had asked for his presence, as there was a remote chance that there might be a firearms incident nearby. Mike didn't particularly like the whole idea and was a bit disconcerted to find himself attending this briefing on his own, but, as there hadn't been any mention of firearms thus far, most probably the worst he'd see were cuts and bruises or maybe a broken bone or two.

While their colleagues went downstairs, Phil and Andy walked over to Mike, introduced themselves and offered him a cup of tea. He recognised the two men from the briefing, during which they'd been referred to as the crew of the ARV, whatever that was, although it couldn't have been that important as they, too, were on standby at Consett.

Elsewhere, it wasn't just the police who were up early; the officers of Derwentside District Council, too, had rolled out of their beds at the crack of dawn, as had the members of the press. The whole juggernaut was juddering slowly into gear, picking up speed as it travelled inexorably to its tragic conclusion.

Mike Peckett had just been hired by local newspaper the *Northern Echo* as a photographer and was on the lookout to make a name for himself. He'd been assigned to cover the Dryden story, as his editor thought that there might be some good pictures to be had. He didn't have much of a clue as to where Butsfield was, though, so that morning he called at his mother's house at Anfield Plain, just outside Durham, to ask her for directions. As well as giving him a much-needed cup of tea at that time of the morning, she was able to tell him precisely where the bungalow was and, without prompting, told him that Dryden was a well-known local eccentric, giving her son some background information on the man and the campaign he'd been waging over his bungalow. She asked Mike to be careful, too, as she was worried that Dryden had a liking for guns and rockets and might be inclined to use them that morning, in light of all his threats. Mike, however, took this as no more than a mother's natural concern and, reassuring her that he'd look after himself, set out to find Eliza Lane.

He arrived at Butsfield at around 7.45am (he was, in fact, the first of the press to arrive), whereupon he found Dryden pottering around his field. Dryden had been up for most of the night, thinking about the next morning's confrontation, although any preparations he might have made weren't evident, apart from a chain that he'd secured around the gate on to the land and a board to which two official-looking letters had been pinned.

Mike, never shy, scaled the fence, walked over to Dryden and began chatting to him. He introduced himself as a photographer from the *Northern Echo* and told him that a journalist would be along shortly. He found Dryden to be amiable, friendly and co-operative (if mildly eccentric), chattering on as he collected eggs from some chickens who were laying within the bungalow. Mike also thought he saw some goats in there and wondered what else was inside this mini-Noah's Ark. He unslung his cameras and began to take some preliminary background photographs, and before long journalists from other newspapers began to arrive, including Garry Willey of the *Evening Chronicle* and Anne Taylor of *The Journal*.

As the press presence grew, Dryden became more pumped up, and when Mark Summers – the reporter from the *Northern Echo* – arrived to add words to Mike's pictures, he was stopped by Garry Willey as he set off towards his colleagues. 'Don't do anything to upset him,' Garry warned. 'He's hyper.'

Mark had had dealings with Dryden over a long period

of time, though, and promptly leaned over the fence and greeted him, asking, 'Can I come on your land?'

Dryden readily agreed but said, 'When I give the warning, I'm going to clear my land. You go running.'

As a veteran of council skirmishes with the public and the inevitable threats and posturing involved, Summers didn't place too much emphasis on Dryden's warning when he climbed over the fence to join him. As he did so, he caught sight of Dryden's band of supporters and hangers-on, even recognising a few of them, including two he knew to be Dryden's closest friends: John Graham and George Cameron.

Then a hush descended on the crowd as the low-loader carrying the digger turned into Eliza Lane from the A68 and parked near the elegant arched entrance to Dryden's property. It was followed by two marked police cars, which parked at the entrance to the lane.

In one of the cars was Inspector Young, and as he pulled up he was instantly annoyed that the press had beaten them to it and had seemingly abandoned their cars all over the lane, so he immediately set about making sure that any further vehicles turning up wouldn't compromise safety by positioning two officers on the lane to control traffic. As he got out of the back seat of his car, Steven Campbell anticipated that he'd just be spending an easy couple of hours standing in the sun, keeping an eye on proceedings, and would be back before the canteen closed. And, if Dryden caused any trouble, they could arrest him and get back to the police station even quicker.

By this time, there was quite a media scrum going on down by the gate, where Dryden was holding court. The sergeant in charge there, a tall, spare man also named Campbell (first name Colin), walked slowly down the lane towards Dryden. As he passed, he eyed the press nervously, having already told his namesake, 'I don't want to get caught on camera if I can help it.'

Dryden acknowledged the sergeant as someone he'd known for years. The two locked eyes and Colin said, 'Now, I don't want no trouble, Albert.'

Dryden replied, 'Oh, there'll be no trouble.'

There was a pause, and then Campbell dropped his gaze and nodded gravely before turning away and strolling back to give his report to Inspector Young.

As Campbell walked away, Dryden was heard by those around him to mutter under his breath that he was prepared to shoot people if they tried to knock down his bungalow. Everyone seemed to take this as a show of bravado on Dryden's part, but Mike Peckett remembers joking back with him, 'Look, don't shoot the bloke in the blue jumper.' Needless to say, he was the bloke in the blue jumper.

Mark Summers watched this exchange and recalls, 'At the back of my mind, knowing what he'd said in the past, I had an uneasy feeling. "What's going to happen? When he's talked the talk, will he walk the walk?" But I thought, "No, no, no. The police are there and the TV cameras have turned up." I thought no man in his right mind would do anything with that presence. It would just be ludicrous.'

Back at the council depot, too, things were gearing up for the assault on Butsfield. Only two men would be needed for the job, but the first two who were selected were excused on account of being friends with Dryden and uncomfortable about the task in hand. The next two also wanted to refuse, protesting that it wasn't their kind of work and that they were concerned about the rumours of possible violence that had been circulating. After being threatened with suspension they finally agreed to go – under protest – whereupon they were presented with hard hats and a pair of boltcutters and sent on their way, having been instructed to remove any valuables from the buildings before they were demolished.

At that hour of the morning, Harry Collinson was still in his office, checking the last-minute arrangements. He rang the depot and told the supervisor that he would meet the men at Butsfield, then called Michael Dunstan, the council's solicitor, who confirmed that he would be there, too. Harry planned to be back by lunchtime, so he slid his sandwich box into his desk drawer, stood up, looked around, picked up the file, his coat and his hard hat and made his way down to his car.

EIGHT

As he turned right into Eliza Lane, Harry passed the police cars stationed at the junction and was stopped by a constable, to whom he identified himself and was waved through. He parked his car on the grass verge at the top of the lane, got out, donned his coat and hard hat and picked up his file, then looked down the lane to see a crowd milling about around the gateway into Dryden's field.

Harry walked down to the gate, approaching on the opposite side of the road, trying not to draw attention to himself, until he drew level with the digger. He could hear Dryden protesting the injustice of the demolition process to his entourage and the reporters. Harry wasn't interested in that sort of thing; he just wanted to get his job done as quickly, quietly and professionally as possible.

First of all, Harry walked over to the driver of the digger

and discussed with him the best way of getting the cumbersome machine on to the site. Between them, they agreed that the least damage would be caused by going through the fence further down the lane if Dryden wouldn't let them through the gate, which was fixed to a large ornamental brick arch that might have to be knocked down in order to accommodate the earthmoving equipment. A ditch in front of the fence concerned Harry, but it didn't seem to bother the digger driver.

Meanwhile, over by the gate itself there was a BBC camera team consisting of a reporter, cameraman and soundman, who were conducting an interview with Dryden. The reporter, Tony Belmont, a familiar figure on North-East TV, wasn't really meant to be there and, instead, should have been in Newcastle, reading the news; he was covering for a colleague who had another commitment. Now here he was, out in the wilds, talking to some crazy old man who thought he was a Wild West frontiersman.

There certainly seemed to be sufficient interest in what was going on, judging by the number of press people thronging at the gate. It was almost as if the BBC had been expressly summoned there by Derwentside District Council. But it wasn't exactly a headline story. It was just one of those stories that might make it as a filler in the local news but was more likely to end up on the cutting-room floor.

Whatever the reason for his presence, Tony was here now, so he might as well make the effort and hear what Dryden had to say. The would-be farmer certainly looked the part of an eccentric, clad in a checked sports jacket, a baseball cap and a grey, matted, straggly beard, while his bungalow — if that was what it was meant to be — was full of animals. Tony moved closer to Dryden, motioning his crew to follow, and joined the huddle of reporters crowding around him. The questioning was relentless, but the old man seemed to be revelling in it, relishing his fifteen minutes of fame.

'... and I hope they haven't got the bloody stupidity to go in there,' Tony heard as he walked closer.

'They say they're going to ask you if they can demolish your bungalow,' another reporter chimed in.

'Well, the answer will be no,' Dryden replied emphatically. 'There's an appeal in, and there's an inspector from the Department of the Environment coming out. One of Heseltine's men. In five weeks' time — and if the inspector makes a decision that it's got to come down, it will probably be eight weeks from now — I'll take it down.'

Tony manoeuvred skilfully to the front of the posse. 'What sort of resistance have you put up this morning?' he asked.

'Well, nothing really,' admitted Dryden. 'Everything seems to be all right. It's just normal, you know?'

Pointing to the padlock and chains, Tony added, 'I see you've got the gate locked here.'

'Well, that's on the instruction of my solicitor, see, and there's an appeal there,' said Dryden, leaning over the gate to indicate the two letters pinned to the board. 'See? It's all in order. There's a letter from my solicitor, you see. And it's a bad job if they can't wait five weeks for the inspector to make his decision. That's all we want.'

'What other measures have you taken this morning to keep them out?' persisted Tony, angling to draw Dryden out. Pictures of pieces of paper were hardly riveting journalism. If that was all he was going to get, he might as well have stayed at home.

'I haven't took any other measures,' stated Dryden. 'As I say, this is private property and there's two gates on here, and they've trespassed on a number of occasions. We've had Mr Collinson to the Crown Court recently, and he has to go back again, with Mr Wright, the enforcement officer. He's going up on four charges. Then Mr Wright and Mr Collinson again.'

As he rambled on in this fashion, Dryden was looking around at the reporters and their crews assembled in front of him. This was his moment and he was determined to make the most of it. He kept hold of the lapels of his jacket like a barrister pontificating on a point of law in the High Court.

Then Tony Belmont enquired, 'Do you accept that the bungalow has to come down eventually?'

'No, no. Well, I don't know, really. This decision will be made by the Secretary of State, not me, and not the council.'

'And what if the Secretary of State says it has to come down?'

'Ah, well, if he says it has to come down, I'll take it down. That's all we're waiting for now. We think we're entitled to this appeal, and he knows we are. And if he's prepared to travel 328 miles to the site in five weeks' time, then he'll go back and make a decision and I'll get a letter and the council'll get a letter, and that decision then stands.'

Where Dryden had got the idea that a Department of the Environment inspector was coming to visit him was a mystery, as at this stage there'd been no indication that this would happen. And why, Tony wondered, was Dryden so precise about the mileage involved? However, hearing little of interest from Dryden, he cut him short, concluding the interview with: 'Lovely, thanks very much.'

At this, Dryden bridled, puffed out his chest like a fighting cock and, with a self-satisfied smile, looked directly into the camera and said, 'But there's only one thing: the council aren't going to win. I know that; I've information that I can't reveal to you, but I know this time I'll keep it.'

The gathered newshounds wondered exactly what Dryden meant by that, but they were then distracted when Harry Collinson moved towards the gate under the arch behind which Dryden was standing. The crowd of onlookers seemed to swell and pressed ominously as Harry got closer, before stopping only a couple of feet away. The press, council workmen, Dryden's supporters and Sergeant Colin Campbell kept a close and watchful eye on proceedings, and out of the corner of his eye Harry could see that Michael Dunstan had arrived and was watching proceedings from a discreet vantage point on the other side of the road. Harry was relieved, as there was always the possibility that Dryden might try to throw a legal spanner in the works at the eleventh hour. He turned his attention back to Dryden and began to talk to him in reasoned tones. 'We'd like to go through the gate, if you'll open it.'

'Why do you want to go through the gate?' Dryden countered.

'You know we've got an enforcement notice which is valid.'

'Well, I want you to read that,' said Dryden, pointing to the papers stapled to the gate. 'That's an official letter. There's an appeal in, and there's an inspector coming out on this site in five weeks' time, right? He'll go back and make a decision.'

Harry knelt down and examined the document studiously. 'It doesn't say that, Albert. Where does it say that?'

'Well, I have another letter confirming that.'

'Can I see the other letter?'

'I'm not going to show you the other letter. This chap is coming out in five weeks' time.'

'You have another letter?'

'I have a letter.'

'Can you show me that letter?' he repeated.

'No, because it's in the hands of my solicitor and he's coming sometime this morning. There's an inspector coming out on this site without doubt, and if you take the law into your own hands you'll be charged with criminal damage. All I'm asking is to wait five weeks for the outcome, maybe six. It'll take a week after he's been out.'

Dryden spoke slowly, but somehow he never seemed to draw breath. He just stood there, gazing into Collinson's eyes with his hands firmly thrust into his pockets, willing him to back down.

It would be a matter of record that his solicitor never attended the site that day.

Collinson glared back at Dryden and said, 'I'm satisfied, Albert, that there's nothing in these documents that affects the legality of this enforcement notice that the inspector has confirmed.'

'Well, there is, Harry,' retorted Dryden, lapsing back into first-name terms. He indicated the arch above them and continued, 'And if you come through them gates, you'll be charged with criminal damage. And if you knock that down, you'll have £40,000 to pay out of your own money when you go to the Crown Court.'

Collinson had nothing to lose and, in the hope that it might mollify Dryden, conceded, 'OK, because of the arch you've got there, we're not going to try and come through the gate.'

Dryden was defiant. 'Well, you're not going through the fence and ploughing all those trees down.'

'We'll go through the fence if you don't open the gate,' Harry insisted. 'We'll obviously have to take the fence down with the machine, so if you want you can have some time to remove the fence yourself to minimise the damage. Do you want to do that?'

Dryden started prodding his finger towards Collinson, his manner more determined than ever and a wild fire leaping in his eyes. 'No. No, I'm asking you one more time to let this appeal go through, and I'm asking you to wait five weeks. If you don't, you'll have to suffer the consequences.' His first threat.

'We can't wait for ever.'

'Well, that's up to you.'

'May we or may we not come through?'

'There's livestock in the house – three goats, sixteen hens,' Dryden protested. Harry felt that this was progress, as he was at least talking about removing the livestock.

Dryden then turned behind him to where his group of supporters was standing, milling amongst the reporters. 'John?' he prompted.

'Yeah, correct,' responded John Graham.

Sensing an opportunity, Harry changed tack. 'Can I just explain this to you, Albert?' he asked

'The RSPCA will be here shortly,' Dryden replied.

'OK, if we gain entry to the site with the machine, you know the purpose of the machine is to demolish the bungalow?'

'You're not.'

'And the other buildings.'

'You're not coming through there. That's criminal damage. All of them trees – it took ten years for all of them trees to grow. I'm not having them flattened.'

Harry listened to this, dropped his head and, with a sigh, said, 'Can I just say that …'

'The council encourage people to plant trees, for screening,' Dryden interrupted. 'Now you… All the work – ten years' work, I've done; ten years' work, nearly, you're going to flatten.'

'Well, that wouldn't be necessary if you'd complied with the enforcement notice.'

'And what about the preservation order on them beech trees? You can't knock any of them down.'

'Right.'

'There's a preservation order. You're breaking the law yourself.'

'Can I just explain about the livestock?' asked Harry, determined to regain control of the conversation.

'You can explain what you like,' sniffed Dryden.

'If we gain entry to the site with the machine, then we'll take the livestock out of the building.'

'You won't take the livestock out of the building,' said Dryden, and as if on cue the crowing of a cockerel sounded loudly in the background, prompting a ripple of laughter from the throng around him.

Harry continued, 'And if you obstruct us in trying to do this, then you appreciate that any damage subsequently caused as a result of your preventing us doing that will be your liability?'

Dryden briefly glanced around him as if to ensure that the whole company's entire attention was focused on him. He fixed Harry Collinson with a stare and said slowly, 'Well, you might not be around to see the outcome of this disaster. Now you've been warned.'

It was almost as if time had been suspended. The stress in Dryden's threat was on the word *you*. What else could his chilling words be but a direct threat to Harry Collinson's life? But was it just the bravado of a man playing to his audience, or was this the final ultimatum of a man pushed to his limit? No one who heard him that day was absolutely sure.

His mouth suddenly dry, Harry asked him, 'Can you explain what you mean by that, Albert?'

Like a man who had made a decision from which he could not back down, Dryden said, 'I'm not going to explain, but if you had any sense you'd go away now. Wait five weeks for the outcome of that,' he said, glancing at the notice. 'That's me last word on it.'

The moment was broken and there was an almost audible sigh of relief, but the reporters standing beside Dryden, including Garry Willey and Anne Taylor, started to scribble furiously in their notebooks while Mike Peckett leaned forward to take some close-ups of Dryden, who seemed for all the world like he was used to being lionised by the press and was savouring every moment of it.

Nobody could tell what Harry was thinking as he said, 'If you can show me the letter referring to the five weeks, we'll consider it.'

Dryden replied, 'I've told you where the letter is. An inspector is coming out in five weeks' time and I'm asking the council to wait 'til he's been out and made his decision. If the inspector says the house or the bungalow or the summerhouse has to come down, then I'll take it down.'

At this point, Dryden moved closer to Harry until their

faces were inches apart. Something in his manner had changed. 'But I'm going to tell you something: this time I'm gonna win. When the inspector comes out, I'm gonna be allowed to keep it for livestock and storage. I'm gonna win and I'll give you ninety to one, but I'm asking you to wait five weeks and if the outcome of the inquiry – the meeting – when he comes up here and he writes to you an official letter and says, "Mr Collinson, the summerhouse or bungalow has to come down," I'll take it down, brick by brick.'

His confidence returning, Harry made his final offer, 'If you produce the letter, we'll read it but, until the letter is produced, we'll go through the fence down the road. And, as I've said, if you want time to remove the fence…'

At this point, Dryden made his next threat: 'Well, you do so at your own risk.'

'But if you don't remove it yourself,' Harry continued, undeterred, 'we'll have to remove it with the machine.'

The cock in the building crowed again and Dryden repeated, 'You do so at your own risk. It's entirely up to you.'

After the briefest of pauses, Harry uttered an authoritative 'Right.'

'But you're making a sad decision,' said Dryden, his hands in his pockets as the cock crowed a third time, watching Harry Collinson, as he turned his back and walked across the road to where Michael Dunstan was waiting.

Amongst the crowd that day was Dryden's nephew, Simon Donnelly, who watched as Collinson paused for a moment before he turned. As he did so, a feeling crept over him that he was witnessing a man about to meet his fate. There was almost a sense of resignation about him and, for the first time, Simon thought, 'This could go seriously wrong.'

After Harry had relayed in detail to Dunstan what had happened at the gate, the pair discussed that morning's progress of the situation so far and came to the conclusion that they would be unable to demolish the bungalow with Dryden's consent. This left two options: to give up or to continue in the face of resistance until things became unworkable.

'You know we're not going to resolve this by negotiation,' said Dunstan. 'We've got to take the next step forward, which is the starting of the process.'

Harry knew that the solicitor was right. Both he and Dryden had played their final cards, and now there was no going back. The shame of it was that Harry took no pleasure in what he was about to do; he just wished that there was another way.

Moving into the centre of the road, Harry gestured at the driver of the low-loader, who drove further down the lane in order to unload the bulldozer at the location where they'd planned to enter the site through the fence. The vehicle moved ponderously forward and Harry went over to wait by the fence as it was unloaded.

As soon as the bulldozer was off the truck, waiting only for Harry's command, John Graham walked over to it. He climbed up, opened the driver's door of the cab and asked the driver not to go any further, but he received the time-honoured response from the clearly embarrassed driver: 'I'm only doing what I'm told.'

Graham then began to harangue Collinson, arguing, 'It's gonna start a whole load of trouble in Consett. It's gonna start up a hell of a lot of trouble!'

Harry tried to interject, but Graham continued, 'Don't think just 'cause there's a few of us today... There's a lot of people behind Albert; there's a lot of people behind the man, causing a hell of a lot of trouble in the district, that's for sure.'

As Graham and Harry were speaking, Dryden had been watching the low-loader's progress down Eliza Lane with a fixed stare, his jaw set, as the bulldozer was unloaded. By this time, most of the press had gravitated towards Collinson, leaving Dryden isolated at the gate. As the attention moved its focus away from him, there was a visible change as he reached a decision.

Dryden turned on his heel and strode slowly towards the far side of the caravan, took off his jacket, folded it carefully and put it just inside the open door. Observed by only a few, he then reached under the wheel arch and withdrew a western-style gun belt, which he then unravelled and buckled over his jumper. Had anyone been looking at him at this point, they would have seen that there was a gun in the holster. Like a gunfighter in a cheap spaghetti western, Dryden tightened the cinch around his thigh, then began to walk over towards the fence where Collinson was standing.

Down in Eliza Lane, Graham was still berating Collinson.

'So he built that house without permission?' queried Graham.

'He built the house without permission.'

'That's not what we heard, mind. He had permission.'

'John, you know perfectly well…'

'Why would you let him build the house? Fair enough, take the top two or three courses of bricks off the bottom and build a house right to the top. We don't do things like that. Only Germans do things like that.'

By now, his supporters and the crowd of press inside the fence could see Dryden's approach. The whole episode was beginning to take on a surreal quality, the feeling of a drama being played out in slow motion. The gun belt and its contents were evident – people remember seeing it – but it was just an actor's prop. A dreamlike atmosphere had seemed to settle on the gathering – not even a sense of disbelief; more a sense that belief had been suspended in time. This was the next stage in the strategy of threats. Dryden had simply notched up the stakes. That was all.

Somebody called out, 'What happens now, Albert?'

Dryden made no response as he strode on, closing the gap between him and Collinson.

Mike Peckett, the man in the blue jumper who didn't want to get shot, was more convinced than most about the little man's purpose and twice urged Dryden that he didn't need a gun to help him state his case.

Meanwhile, Dryden's nephew, Simon Donnelly, could see the resolve in his uncle's eye and called to him, 'Take all that off! You don't need any of that!' He knew well that, when he had an idea in his head, Uncle Albert wasn't a man to be thwarted.

It was as if Dryden hadn't even heard them, even though they were only a few feet away. He looked neither to the left nor to the right but maintained his steady pace, his eyes focused firmly on Collinson. Most believed the pistol only to be a replica or, at best, not loaded. None believed that Dryden intended to use it. In fact, it was the pistol he'd bought from his school friend so many years before, the weapon that had caused the groove in his scalp. The Webley revolver.

When Dryden got to within ten paces of Collinson, he stopped, his feet slightly apart. Only then did he look around him, as if to check that everyone was taking notice, and indeed by that point he had everyone's attention – everyone's, that is, except that of Collinson and John Graham, who were still bickering on the other side of the fence.

Dryden slowly drew his weapon from its holster with his right hand and lifted it in front of him, away from his body, pointing at the ground. Then he moved his left hand over to the gun and, using the thumb of that hand, slowly drew back the hammer until it clicked, exposing the firing pin. The pistol was now in single-action mode, reducing the trigger pressure necessary to fire it from 14lb per square inch to only 2.5lb per square inch – just a whisper of a squeeze. Then Dryden moved forward a couple of paces. Nobody breathed.

Collinson and John Graham, meanwhile, were still arguing hotly.

'John, you know perfectly well that Albert dug a big hole so that the bungalow was built in the hole, so that the thing could be finished,' said Collinson, exasperated.

'What about the roof? *What about the roof?* It's about... that – that too much high,' said Graham, demonstrate a 4in gap with his fingers, 'and this hassle's just about a little bit of cement.'

'John, you know perfectly well...'

But then John interrupted him. 'Hey up,' he said, noticing Dryden for the first time.

Albert Dryden was standing with the revolver held out before him, as if helpfully posing for the photographers. He looked unhurriedly from left to right, ensuring that he was the centre of everyone's attention. He wasn't flustered; indeed, he appeared quite calm.

Collinson, hands on hips, seemingly composed, spoke to the BBC cameraman standing nearby: 'Can you get a shot of this gun?'

This seemed to prompt Dryden into action. He lifted the weapon with a straight arm to head height and pointed it at Collinson, who was by now only feet away. He looked over the sights and slowly squeezed the trigger.

There was a small, almost insignificant *crack!* as the gun went off. Someone said later, 'It quite surprised me. You hear guns on movies and think of large noises when guns go off, but it wasn't anything like that. It was a very small sound.' Others had thought Dryden had fired a blank, but of course he hadn't. He'd fired the real thing – a solid fragment of lead that, with a speed that defied sight, flew straight and true and struck its target.

Without a sound, Harry Collinson fell on to his back into the drainage ditch, his arms spread in a grotesque parody of a crucifix as his fingers grasped feebly at the long grass for an instant and then were still.

NINE

It was like the final word of the final scene of a play, where the audience hold their anticipation for one short second before bursting into applause.

For a split second, nobody moved on the field. Then the brief hiatus of calm before the full realisation of what had happened broke and gave way to pandemonium. People began to run – some screaming – trying to put distance between themselves and this deranged psychopath who had so calmly struck down an unarmed man without even a flicker of emotion.

The press, too, scattered. They hadn't turned up for this. A good, newsworthy row, yes, perhaps even a few blows traded to liven matters up, but this was beyond all comprehension.

No one present had ever seen a gun fired in anger

before, and very few would otherwise have ever seen a man die before their eyes, especially not in such violent circumstances. As they ran blindly, they were convinced that they were running for their lives.

Meanwhile, Dryden had quickly cocked the weapon again, moved forward and ducked through the rails of the fence. Without a second glance, he stepped over Collinson's inert body towards the centre of Eliza Lane. Mike Peckett was kneeling close to Collinson's body, his mind a blank, not sure whether the council official was alive or dead but feeling that he should comfort him, and then Dryden turned towards him, still with the loaded weapon in his hand.

Peckett was terrified. 'Look,' he blustered, 'you don't need to shoot me. I'm not involved in this!'

Dryden's eyes locked with Peckett's for a moment and then moved on, not remotely interested in him.

Peckett ran to take cover behind the closest car, his cameras clanking around his neck, his breath coming in short gasps as he fought to quell the fear that threatened to suffocate him. He crouched down, squeezing behind the car, praying that Dryden wouldn't come his way. His thoughts were racing and he expected to see the barrel of a gun pointing towards his face at any moment, worried that Dryden might have thought he was giving succour to the dying man and would seek revenge. 'I was very upset about the fact that I was even looking at someone who had been killed,' he confessed later. 'I couldn't even understand why he had been killed.' He was only too aware that his blue jumper wouldn't save him from a bullet if one should come his way.

Some of Dryden's friends and supporters were still nearby. One of them – possibly his old school friend George Cameron – hoping to prevent further tragedy, called out, 'Albert, Albert, Albert son,' while John Graham, as he tried to get out of the way, yelled, 'Oh my God! Whoa, whoa, whoa!'

The crowd was galvanised into action, jostling and pushing each other in their haste to escape, and the scene was one of utter chaos, with journalists, council workmen and police officers fleeing for their lives up the lane to the main road. The press crews were severely hampered by their gear, but their instinct for survival gave wings to their feet. People were shouting at each other, all pretence at politeness having been abandoned. The cameras were still running, snapping blindly at tarmac and sky, and tape recorders were still running, picking up one particularly desperate individual yelling to his panic-stricken fellow, 'Get out of the fucking way!' Then realisation of events suddenly dawned when someone else said, 'Jesus Christ! He's shot the councillor!' OK, so Harry was a council officer, not a councillor, but who was splitting hairs right now?

Once through the fence, Dryden fired one shot directly across the road at the stationary low-loader (now devoid of its crew, who had also fled), then turned and slowly walked on behind the exodus in front of him. He appeared to be searching for something, or someone, as he scanned the backs of the people in front of him. He thumbed back the hammer on the weapon, aimed and fired again, hitting a man who he'd been talking to earlier: BBC reporter Tony Belmont, who was hit in the left arm, which immediately dropped, useless, by his side.

Why Tony? What had he said to enrage Dryden so much that he wanted to kill him? Despite his wound, Belmont carried on up the lane, away from Dryden.

Then came the crack of another shot, and a scream was heard as PC Steven Campbell was hit in the back. Dryden had even less cause to shoot Steven, having stood in the background behind his sergeant while the action had unfolded. Dryden appeared to be firing indiscriminately into the mêlée – or did he have a particular target in mind?

Dryden paused, turned again and walked back up to Eliza Lane towards Collinson's body. As he made his progress, reloading as he went, he fired wildly into the windscreens of vehicles parked at the side of the road. As he drew level with Collinson's body, he stopped suddenly, as if a thought had just occurred to him, then walked back to the corpse and stood directly over it, straddling the ditch and looking down into Collinson's sightless eyes. With a maddening slowness, and taking deliberate aim, he fired twice in rapid succession, first into Collinson's face and then into his chest, the council worker's lifeless body jerking at each separate impact. Dryden's face was an expressionless mask; in his tortured mind, he was exacting retribution for the unwarranted persecution he'd suffered over the years. Someone had to pay the price, and Harry Collinson deserved to die.

Slowly, Dryden holstered his pistol and shrugged, both hands on his gun belt, surveying his handiwork, then he swung his leg over the body on to the far side of the ditch and clambered back through the fence. Without a second glance down the lane, he began to stroll, almost jauntily, around the far side of his bungalow and back to the caravan. There must have been a certain amount of pride within him that he, Albert Dryden, had saved his homestead from the tyrannical aggressor with whom he had struggled all these months. That would teach anyone else to think twice before they contemplated tangling with him.

As he reached the caravan, Dryden stood a while on the step and watched as a police car turned into Eliza Lane and, after a pause, started to make its way towards him. Then suddenly the driver threw the car into reverse. Shaking his head at this erratic behaviour, Dryden went inside, took off his gun belt, wrapped it carefully around the holster and put it on the shelf. He had made his point; he didn't need it any more – not until the next time, at least. Then, calmly, he boiled the kettle and made himself a mug of tea, crouched down on the step and watched the erstwhile spectators, milling around at the end of the lane like ants whose nest has been disturbed. The sun was beating down. It was a pleasant day.

Down at the end of Eliza Lane, things weren't so calm.

People were rushing headlong, in fear of their lives, and the police were struggling to quell the panic and impose some semblance of order on the situation.

Meanwhile, Tony Belmont — ever the tenacious journalist — was trying to keep things going for the benefit of his viewers. With his left arm hanging limply, dripping blood, he instructed his cameraman to focus on him and then, breathlessly, began to talk: 'Quickly, quickly, me, me. We were standing watching what was going on. The chief planner was trying to persuade the chap to move out of the way and let the digger go in and then a shot rang out and the chief planner fell to the ground, and I felt a shot in the arm and, as you can tell, I've been shot in the arm. And I now hopefully am going to get some medical treatment. A policeman was also shot in the buttock here and the councillor was shot in the chest.' Then the pain took over and Tony moaned, 'Oh, God. Oh, oh, oh.'

Tony sank slowly down to the verge, clutching his arm. A shadow moved in front of him and he heard a voice gently reassuring him, then felt someone gently take hold of his injured arm and lift it above his head. One of the police officers had come over to help and now peeled back his shirtsleeve to reveal the entry wound, just above the elbow, and there was a huge swelling just above Belmont's wrist where the bullet had tracked and finally lodged.

By this time, Belmont was starting to go into shock. The colour had drained from his face and he started to shake and groan. There was no medical help, despite the fact that

114

there'd been a paramedic at the briefing earlier, so the policeman stayed with him, trying to reassure him and make him as comfortable as possible.

Meanwhile, the injured policeman, Steven Campbell, had been helped out of the crowd. (He later remembered feeling only a slight stinging sensation in his lower back as the bullet had struck him.) Someone was holding him up by the arm, and he desperately wanted to sit down. He heard a voice say, 'Can we take this boy somewhere?' and then found himself on the roadside, on his hands and knees, while someone behind him fumbled with the belt of his trousers, trying to get them undone.

By this time, the pain had taken hold and Steven was engulfed by waves of nausea. His shirt, now splashed with a patch of red that was his blood, was pulled up over his back and he felt the cool breeze caressing his back, which, by now, was on fire. Whoever was helping him examined his wound, which consisted only of a small, neat, round hole above his right buttock. Then Steven was in the queue for the paramedic, hoping someone had actually thought to call him. In the meantime, there was little he could do but wait.

By now, it had begun to dawn upon the rest of the journalists that they'd just scooped probably the greatest exclusive of their careers. Garry Willey realised that he had the story of a lifetime and that he had better start getting some quotes while he had the chance, but the police and council workers were too busy to talk to, and there was no one else to interview but other journalists. So began a bizarre merry-go-round with each reporter trying to get a better quote than the one they'd just given. Garry began with the BBC camera crew, and then reciprocated with an interview to camera for them. They were all in a state of shock and breathless, but their professional instincts took over and they made the best of what they had.

As soon as he got to the end of the lane, a traumatised Mike Peckett ran across the main road and jumped into his car, then drove a short distance to the next farmhouse. He battered on the door and explained what had happened to the bewildered housewife who answered and he pleaded with her to let him use the telephone. He was only too well aware of how quickly a story like this could get out, and his first priority was to let his family know that he was alive and unharmed, so he rang his wife and outlined that morning's events. Relieved that he was alive but upset at the thought of what might so easily have happened, Mrs Peckett agreed to ring Mike's mother immediately to let her know that she was safe, bearing in mind her prophetic warnings from earlier that morning.

Mike then telephoned his office in Darlington and told his editor what had happened to turn a fairly routine assignment into a front-page story. When his editor expressed disbelief, Mike shouted angrily down the phone until he gained an incredulous acceptance that what he was telling was, in fact, the truth, that such events really had occurred in the rural charm and tranquillity of County Durham.

Now the editor was eager for the pictures, realising that

the national papers would soon be buzzing around the story and that Peckett's pictures could prove to be a goldmine. He suggested sending someone out to collect Mike's film and getting him back to the scene for more, but Mike told him that he'd come straight back to the office to process what he'd got and that, if he wanted any further coverage, he'd have to send a replacement photographer. He'd had enough; he knew how close he had been to death that morning and wasn't about to go back down Eliza Lane while that madman was on the loose.

Meanwhile, Dryden's nephew, Simon, also didn't want to be there. He just wanted to get away from the scene as quickly as he could, finding it hard to come to terms with what he'd seen his uncle do that morning. His mind was in a whirl. The man who'd pulled the gun that morning – that couldn't possibly be the same man who used to tell him adventure stories as a young child, who had cared for his gran and his disabled uncle, surely? Not that murderer.

Simon felt disloyal, reluctant for anyone – especially the press – to discover his relationship with Dryden. He knew that there was someone he had to tell straight away: his mother. He couldn't bear the idea of her hearing of her brother's bloody deeds from someone else, as the news would affect their whole family. So he climbed into his van and started the engine, forcing himself to concentrate. After everything he'd seen that morning, the last thing he wanted to do was crash.

As he started to drive off the verge, there was a loud banging on the side of the van and Simon stopped, startled as two white, anxious faces appeared at the side window. He recognised them as Derwentside District Council workers who had been at the site and began to wind down the window, but one of them had already opened the door. They begged him to take them with him back to Consett, and Simon, seeing the strain etched on their faces, relented and let them climb into the van.

After a few minutes of strained silence, one of the council workers said, 'I'm glad to be out of there. I'm going on the sick.'

This seemed to encourage the other man, who put in, 'I'm going to the Empire Club for a drink.'

Simon tried to work out which of them had the best idea, but he resolved to go to work and try to put the events of that morning out of his mind. First, though, he had to face his mother.

Unaware of how events were unfolding in Butsfield, Phil Brown, Andy Reay and paramedic Mike Leonard had found their way to the canteen at Consett Police Station and were enjoying a leisurely cup of coffee. The two coppers had their radios on but there didn't seem to be much happening down at the site and, indeed, they'd just been discussing why they needed to be there.

Then Superintendent Hegarty came into the canteen and told them that everything was going to plan and that he didn't think that they'd be needed much longer, adding that, as soon as the council had started to knock down the building, they could go. Hegarty seemed almost apologetic at such an anticlimactic turn of events and disappeared downstairs. Even so, he and Inspector Young made their way out to Butsfield, just to check.

As he left, the ARV crew's thoughts turned to an important matter: food. Early days always made you hungry, and one of the shift's few pleasures was being able to get a cooked breakfast at one of the police canteens, which were renowned for quantity rather than quality.

As they had a roving remit for the north part of the county, Phil and Andy were discussing which station they should go to for their breakfast and suggested to Mike that he might as well join them if he had nothing better to do. The paramedic considered the matter for a moment, but he knew that he had a mountain of paperwork waiting for him on his desk back in Durham and told them that he'd settle for just a coffee. After some earnest discussion, during which they decided that they definitely didn't want to go back to headquarters in Durham, where someone would be sure to find them some more jobs to do, Phil and Andy settled on Chester-le-Street as the best available option.

Then they had to decide what they wanted to eat, as both were trying to lose weight to prepare for their rapidly approaching annual firearms fitness test. Fail that and they'd lose their permits. Although the option of a huge, belly-busting cooked breakfast was extremely attractive, Phil and Andy decided to plump for the more healthy option of scrambled eggs and beans. As Andy Reay's hand hovered over the telephone, ready to dial the number for

Chester-le-Street Police Station and make the order, the radio squawked into life.

All Phil Brown can remember hearing were the words 'He's got a gun! He's got a gun!' From that point on, everything seemed to go pear-shaped. It was difficult to understand what was happening after that, as there were so many garbled voices coming over the radio, but it became obvious that a shooting had taken place, which meant that, in a split second, Phil and Andy's role had changed drastically. Nobody had asked for them, but both knew that they had to get to the scene as fast as possible. They looked at each other wordlessly and realised that this was the reason why they had been trained so relentlessly. There was nothing evidently wrong with their fitness levels as they rushed down the stairs and out into the back yard, jumped into their car and steamed out of the gates with a squeal of tyres, laying down twin streaks of rubber.

Mike Leonard, meanwhile, was left sitting open-mouthed in the canteen, wondering where the two cops had disappeared to. As soon as he realised the reason for their sudden departure, he scrambled out of the building and into his ambulance jeep.

Phil and Andy knew that their arrival at Butsfield was literally a matter of life and death. On this occasion, Andy was driving, although both men were experienced advanced drivers and were well able to handle the heavy vehicle safely and each had confidence in the other's ability to drive safely at high speeds. As Andy ploughed through the traffic, overtaking cars and jumping red lights, Phil picked up the VHF radio handset and contacted the control room, asking the operator to get them immediate authority to draw their firearms and, if necessary, use them. It was obvious that those in the control room knew something of what was going on down at Butsfield, as Assistant Chief Constable Eddie Marchant gave Phil and Andy instant authorisation to use weapons if necessary.

The control-room operators had also contacted the county's second ARV, crewed by two time-served firearms officers, Bill Lister and Dave Appleby, who were conducting a static-goods vehicle check near Chester-le-Street, and ordered them to Butsfield to back up Phil and Andy. Bill and Dave dashed to their car, leaving a bemused French lorry driver with his papers in his hand, staring open-mouthed as they sped past him, sirens blaring.

Back in the first ARV, Phil Brown's thoughts were racing: 'This is Consett. It's a Thursday morning. Things like that don't happen in Consett, for God's sake!' He and Andy were trained for the situation, but the gap between training and reality at that time felt immense. He suddenly felt very lonely; he knew that the tactical advisers and the firearms team wouldn't be far behind, but he and Andy would be first on the scene. They had to make the initial evaluation that would guide everyone else's actions, and there was little room for error. People would have high expectations of them, from the bobbies on the ground to the assistant chief constable back at the control room. Their hearts were pounding, their palms were sweating and they wondered what would greet them when they arrived at the scene.

As they drove down the A68, they could see the cluster of vehicles at the end of Eliza Lane and pulled to a halt just inside the entrance to the lane. Sergeant Colin Campbell, who Phil recognised from the briefing, came over to them and said, 'Stevie and this guy,' indicating Belmont, 'have been shot and Albert Dryden's holed up in the caravan.'

Phil and Andy could see the caravan, just in front of the tree line in a field about 200 yards from where they were standing.

That appeared to be all the briefing they were going to get, as Campbell had already turned away to get to the ambulance, which had followed the ARV, and to direct Mike Leonard to the injured.

At that point, the panic seemed to vanish and, as Phil and Andy walked to the rear of their vehicle, their training and professionalism took over. Popping the boot, they took out the heavy Kevlar body armour – capable of stopping a bullet in its tracks – and slung the vests over their heads, fastening the Velcro straps tight. Then each picked up a black leather gun belt and fastened it around his waist, adjusting it for comfort, and then took out a revolver, swung out the chamber, inserting six cartridges and placing the two spare 6-round speedloaders in their belts.

Phil then picked up the radio while Andy picked up a shotgun, turned it over and ritualistically thumbed eight triple-A cartridges – each containing twelve pea-sized lead balls that turned the sporting gun into a lethal weapon –

into the magazine. He then turned the gun over and gently worked the action backwards and forwards once, smoothly sliding a round into the breech. Both men checked each other's gear and, when they were satisfied that they were both ready, they began their approach to the caravan. There was no sign of their quarry.

Phil eased himself into the driver's seat of the car while Andy got into the passenger side, cradling the shotgun between his knees. Out of habit, Andy's hand strayed to the safety catch to make sure it was on while Phil warily coaxed the engine into life and slowly began to coast down Eliza Lane, leaving the Kevlar-lined doors open for protection.

As they drew level with the gateway, Andy saw Albert Dryden standing at the entrance to the caravan, recognising him from the newspapers. 'That's him!' he exclaimed to Phil. 'Back up. Back up!'

Phil reversed the car at speed until they were about twenty-five yards from the gate. All both men could remember was seeing a scruffy little man wearing a big western-type gun belt and holster as he entered the caravan.

Gingerly, they got out of the vehicle and moved behind it, searching for cover. Across the road, a stone wall marked the boundary of the field directly in front of Dryden's caravan, and they decided that it was their best bet. Phil went first, keeping low until he was secure behind the wall, then turned and waved Andy across.

As soon as both men were safe behind the wall, Phil popped his head up over the top to see what further cover was available. He couldn't see Dryden, though, and so decided that they should continue. One at a time, keeping their bodies close to the top of the wall so as not to skyline themselves, Phil and Andy rolled over into the field beyond. As he rolled, Andy remembered the litany that had been drummed into them over and over again by their instructors (where were *they* now?): 'Think cover. Think cover.' When he looked up, Andy's heart almost stopped: there was no bloody cover whatsoever in the field. He followed Phil through a wide, ninety-degree arc amongst the dense, high summer grass to the fence line just in front of the caravan. They were wired now, jumpy, vigilant for any further sign of Dryden, who had by now disappeared from view.

Phil called out, 'Can you hear us, Mr Dryden?'

'Yes, I can hear you,' came a voice from inside the caravan.

'Can you come out and show us where you are?'

Slowly, Dryden came to the door of his caravan to see Phil and Andy standing only 25–30ft away and about 50ft apart, a position that would give the policemen the optimum field of fire, should Dryden pose any kind of threat. Andy had levelled the shotgun ready, his thumb hovering around the push-through safety catch, sweat dripping into his eyes. God, it was hot!

Standing further along by the fence, Phil cradled his revolver in both hands, his finger damp on the cross-hatched trigger, trying to maintain his concentration and keep the notched sights trained on the door of the caravan. He and Andy both knew the theory; now it was time to put it into practice.

Realising that they could be there for some time, Phil did his job as the man in charge, which was to talk to Dryden. Only one voice. Get him on your side. Neither man wanted to shoot Dryden; the aim was to persuade him to surrender. To this end, they needed a dialogue, a conversation with a killer.

'I'm Phil and this is Andy,' said Phil.

That was good. First-name terms would break the ice and help to build a rapport with Dryden.

By this time, Phil and Andy saw that Dryden had removed his holster but couldn't tell whether or not he had it close. Phil was conscious only of trying to keep him talking, and in his recollection he was babbling. After the event, he remembered little of what he'd said to Dryden, but the man appeared to be responding. However, he vividly recalls that at one stage Dryden looked coolly into his eyes and, nodding at the pistol pointing at his chest, said, 'You might have to use that before the end of the day.' Phil knew that this was true, and the thought of it made his blood run cold.

By this time, Bill Lister and Dave Appleby had arrived in the second ARV, and both found it remarkable that, at the top end of Eliza Lane, while there were a lot of people milling about, there appeared to be no panic and very little sense of urgency. There was an ambulance present, and they could see two people who had been injured, but the scene was so calm that they could have been witnessing a training exercise by the Casualties Union.

Bill and Dave had donned their gear as they drove to

Butsfield – not strictly procedure, but at least they were ready for action as soon as they arrived. When they got out of their car, they spotted Geoff Young, the senior officer, by his white shirt. He hurried over and, as the three started to walk down the lane, he started to brief them on what had happened so far. Then, abruptly, he pointed at the door of the caravan, about 100 yards away, and said, 'There's the caravan. There he is now! He's at the door!' Then he turned around. 'Lads?'

There was a hiss and he looked down. 'What are you doing on the deck, lads? Get up.'

The two firearms men persuaded Geoff to take a slightly more cautious route down the lane, using the available cover. When they'd reached the digger, Geoff climbed up on top of the machine to show them where Dryden was, skylining himself wonderfully and making a superb target of himself. Exasperated, Bill talked him down off the vehicle and he and Dave told Geoff that they'd make their own deployment and would radio him as soon as they were in position.

Bill kicked a bottom rail out of the fence and crawled underneath, and then he and Dave leopard-crawled their way up to within 50ft of the end of the caravan, just inside the fence line, where they carved themselves a scrape to give them some cover. They could see Phil and Andy clearly at the front of the caravan, and through the window they saw Dryden come in and out of their view as Phil talked to him. More importantly, they could see the gun belt, lying on a shelf just inside the door.

Satisfied with their position and that Dryden wasn't going anywhere, Bill and Dave resolved to wait it out as the gunman drank tea and ate marmalade sandwiches. The first containment was on.

TEN

In an abandoned warehouse just outside Durham, Bob Gadd and I were putting the last-minute touches to planning what would be quite a complex exercise. Both he and I are perfectionists and would go to almost any lengths to make any training scenario as realistic as possible, only stopping short of using live ammunition. Every last detail had been taken into account and a few twists had been added, such as losing the lunch break. This exercise would be run in real time, and not only would there not be a break but there wouldn't even be any lunch; feeding his men would be just another logistical problem to be solved by whichever lucky student was picked to run the operation.

The inspectors had arrived in their minibus and were champing at the bit, ready to get going, thankful for a day out of the classroom. I knew that John Taylor and the firearms team were getting geared up and were just about ready to leave HQ, so I rang around to make sure those who were meant to be contributing that day were still available. From an earlier conversation I'd had with Phil Brown (and just what had *that* been about?), I knew that I'd already lost the ARV and really didn't want to lose any more resources or the exercise would be shafted.

I picked up the department's mobile phone – jealously guarded, being one of only three in the county, and as large and about as heavy as a couple of bricks – and dialled the number for the direct line of the newly appointed force press officer, Maxine Cawston, a flame-haired beauty who had set many a copper's pulse racing since she'd arrived at Durham but who was extremely good at her job. When she picked up, I asked her if she'd still be available to call the officer in charge of the exercise we'd be running that day with some spurious press enquiries about the incident, which would help add to the burden of command and increase his stress levels. As Maxine confirmed that she could still take part, she stopped abruptly and, after a pause and a muffled conversation at the other end of the line, she said, 'Hold on. Something's coming up. I don't think I'll be able to help you after all. I think somebody's been shot.'

The phone suddenly went dead and I just gazed stupidly at the silent handset, considering carefully whether or not Maxine was trying to wind me up, as she had a wicked sense of humour. Bemused, I slowly put the phone down, wondering what would happen next. Would she ring back with a laugh? Almost immediately, the telephone rang again and I picked it up quickly to hear an agitated control-room inspector asking me to take the firearms team to Butsfield urgently.

'Why?' I demanded. 'What's happened?'

'Some people have been shot."

That focused my thinking immediately, and a slew of questions raced through my brain. What information did I need? What did I need to prepare for? Had anything else been done already? First things first, though: 'Have we got authority?'

'Yes,' said the inspector. 'The ACC is here now, and he's already given authority to the ARV.'

'Are they there yet?'

'Yes. And the north car is *en route.*'

'OK,' I said. 'I'll need as much information as you've got. As soon as we're under way, I'll contact you again. Make sure there's someone to meet us at the plot. And I want ground plans ASAP.'

I told the inspector that the tactical team were at that moment loading up their van at the armoury. 'Tell them to make their own way out to the site and that I'll meet them there. Where is this place, anyhow?' I'd never even heard of bloody Butsfield, which, it turned out, was only a few miles away from my home.

Next, I told the inspector to start a detailed log of events right now and that I wanted a secure, open radio channel on the force network. I could tell from his peevish tone that he was taken aback by my abrupt manner; who did this sergeant think he was? I took no notice, though. At that time, I was a professional doing my job and was prepared to step on as many toes as necessary to get it done properly.

I put down the phone and turned to Bob Gadd. 'We've got a live one,' I told him. 'A place called Butsfield. Somebody's been shot.'

We'd both worked together for long enough and shared enough hair-raising moments to know each other pretty well, and Bob understood immediately that this wasn't part of the exercise. Without waiting for further details, he raced for the car while I told the assembled inspectors to pack up and follow him, as they might just get their most valuable firearms lesson ever and might even prove to be of some use. The only person left was the first aider, who, dumbfounded, was suddenly promoted to being in charge of all the left-behind kit.

Bob was a longtime traffic man and supremely confident behind the wheel, and that morning he needed all his skills as he drove the unmarked blue Astra at high speed towards the centre of Durham. At that point, he had only a vague idea where he was going while the control room radioed in further directions. We burned through the city-centre streets at speeds in excess of 100mph, a hastily penned 'POLICE' sign stuck to the car's front window but without the benefit of blue lights or sirens. It was a pretty hairy ride.

While Bob drove, I tried to maintain communication

with the control room to keep abreast of events as well as direct Bob and work out personnel deployments so I could hit the ground running and get an effective containment in place as soon as possible. I was aware just how vulnerable and out on a limb the ARV men would be feeling by now.

As we raced through the streets of Durham, it was a heart-stopping ride until we'd worked our way through the villages and on to the A68.

We spotted the scene well before arriving there by the cluster of vehicles at the end of Eliza Lane.

Meanwhile, back at the police station, the firearms team had been loading their van outside the armoury when an out-of-breath, dishevelled control-room comms operator came crashing through the double doors. Everyone stopped what they were doing and looked around.

'Sergeant Taylor,' said the comms operator. 'Where's Sergeant Taylor?'

'He's in the armoury,' replied one of the team, indicating the open door.

The man rushed on and collided with John Taylor, who'd been issuing ammunition until he'd heard his name. 'What's up?' he enquired. 'Where's the fire?' He then listened, his brow creasing as the comms operator told him of the happenings at Consett and informed him that I'd asked for his team to go straight to Butsfield. John was a veteran of police firearms and had been around them all his working life, in the navy before his time in the police. He was a powerful, balding man who'd cultivated the dour, unforgiving nature of a grumpy old man, but his face could light up in an instant to reveal an intelligent, witty and surprisingly sensitive side, seen only by a few.

Now John thought through possible strategies and tried to second-guess what Bob and I might need. He called his team back into the armoury and gave them a quick briefing, then the training rounds were exchanged for operational ones, the revolvers for self-loading pistols, and two men were each issued with a 5.56mm Steyr specialist sniper rifle.

Last of all, John called three of the most experienced men to one side. Together with him, they would form an assault team, if necessary. They each took a 9mm Heckler & Koch MP5 carbine, along with two thirty-round magazines, in addition to their regular sidearms.

The laughing and joking that the firearms team had engaged in while loading up their van the first time had been replaced by a sombre, introspective mood. Everything was made ready – magazines filled, weapons loaded and actions checked – all with a quiet and quick efficiency.

One member of the team, a time-served firearms officer named Ian Knight, had worked in the area for a considerable time, although no one had asked him about Albert Dryden. Indeed, not much information had been given out, but Ian instinctively knew it had to be him. His first thought was that the poor bugger had been pushed over the edge and retaliated in the only way he knew. He almost felt sympathy for him, but he pushed it to the back of his mind.

Once the shooter's identity had been confirmed, Ian, in his trademark gravelly voice, gave a pen picture of Dryden to the rest of the team as they travelled, along with a rough layout of the operation. As he directed the driver to take the shortest route, there was a taut, respectful silence. Ian knew that some members of the team had never been involved in a live incident before, and he remembered what it had been like for him that first time, many years earlier. But he was also aware that they were there to do a job: to catch a killer, or even to kill him.

By now, Bob and I were in a complete radio patch with John, and when we turned into Eliza Lane we were greeted by parked vehicles and confusion; there didn't appear to be a rendezvous point, or indeed any control at all. This was something we definitely didn't need, so we slowly weaved our way through to the far side and stopped behind the ARV, where we saw a solitary figure – obviously a policeman, wearing a white shirt and the uniform cap of a senior officer – walking down the centre of the road, apparently unconcerned. We waited until he was parallel with us before getting out of the car, at which point I could identify an exhausted Stan Hegarty – pallid, grey and with an almost vacant look in his eyes.

'Where is this guy?' I asked Hegarty immediately. No niceties or preliminaries; I wanted information, and I wanted it fast.

'Over there,' Hegarty said, nodding towards the caravan, some 40 or 50 yards away.

'What's he got?' asked Bob.

This seemed to jerk a response from Hegarty: 'We think he might have some sort of automatic weapon.'

Just as when the second ARV had arrived, Hegarty suddenly found himself alone, looking around in surprise as Bob and I disappeared, having taken cover behind the same stone wall on the far side of the road. Bob reached out and grabbed Stan Hegarty (who, it was by this time obvious, was severely traumatised) by the arm, pulling him down behind the wall.

Slowly, I began to draw out the story from Hegarty. The body of a man who'd been shot lay in a nearby ditch. The man who'd shot him was sitting on the step of the caravan in an adjacent field, being covered by PC Andy Reay and Acting Sergeant Phil Brown, who were in the field to the right. The other ARV men were ahead of them.

I decided I could get to the body while safely in cover, in order to get some indication as to what sort of weapon the shooter had; after all, if it *was* an automatic, we were in a whole different ball game. Following the line of the wall, I moved gingerly towards Collinson's corpse, which I could see lying in the ditch ahead. Belly flat to the ground, I crawled quickly across the gate opening and along the ditch to the body. I checked behind me nervously, but I was behind any line of fire that might come from the direction of the caravan.

When I reached the body, a quick examination yielded no surprises; I'd seen enough dead bodies in my time. There was one identifiable entry wound, at the chin, although there was evidence of two further shots to the chest, which were obscured by clothing. Only one of these chest wounds was surrounded by a patch of blood, which indicated that it had probably been the first round fired into his body and the primary cause of death. It also looked as though the other two shots had been fired from above as Collinson lay on the ground. Judging by the small entry wound on his face, it looked like Dryden had a 9mm weapon, which could have been either an automatic or a semi-automatic weapon.

Retracing my steps, I crept back to Bob and Stan and then crouched down beside them. While I'd been away, Bob had been able to confirm the exact locations of the four officers on the ground, and we could now hear Phil Brown's muffled conversation with Dryden. Things seemed to be going well. By using the repeater system on the radio in the ARV, they'd set up a direct communications link so that they could talk to all the other officers in the field, while their conversation was relayed back to the control room.

After we'd tactfully asked Hegarty if he wouldn't mind making his way back to the junction, please, to set up a control point from which the operation could be run, Bob and I began to sort out the planning. Bob sketched out the scene, designating the front of the caravan, where Phil and Andy were in cover, as the white side, the rear as black, the left side (where Bill Lister and Dave Appleby were scrunched down) as green and the right as the red side.

We then began to sort out the preliminary deployments, bearing in mind available cover and the need for safe lines of fire, while I considered the tactical options. Actually, I'd already decided on an immediate action plan, if things turned critical and Dryden posed a serious threat: I'd tell Dave to shoot a ferret cartridge, filled with CS gas, from his shotgun through the window on the green side of the caravan to force Dryden out of the front door, directly into Andy and Phil's line of fire. Once I'd told them all of the plan over the radio, I took a look at the containment options that Bob had drawn up.

Just then, the firearms team arrived, coming to a halt on the far side of the bulldozer, having approached slowly from the other end of Eliza Lane. I made my way over to them, relieved to see John and the rest of the guys at last. As they got out of the van, the two uniformed officers who'd been on traffic-control duties at the far end of the lane came over and tried to nab some ballistic vests and helmets, but John shooed them away; his team would need every bit of kit they had.

Along with the rest of their gear, John's team also put on heavy ballistic helmets, an unusual measure (you never put one of those on unless you had to) that demonstrated just how seriously they were treating the incident.

When they were ready, I gathered them around and briefed them. The immediate action plan would stay the same, but I ordered snipers to be put on the red and white sides of the caravan, with a designated killing ground in the front. Meanwhile, the rest of the team were to be positioned in pairs around the caravan in order to provide a 50-yard containment zone in case Dryden did have an automatic weapon and came out blasting.

Ian Knight then went over what he knew about Dryden, which helped me to build up a profile of the subject. And then the time for questions was over, and the officers began to move stealthily into position.

Just then, my radio crackled into life and Bill Lister came on the air with information about Dryden's pistol, which he could see inside the caravan. It seemed to Bill that Dryden's gun wasn't an automatic after all, although this was by no means conclusive. Even if it wasn't, it didn't mean we were out of the woods – not by a long chalk.

The one advantage the firearms team had over the rest of the officers in the field was that they had their own dedicated communications system, which meant that their chain of command wouldn't be compromised by senior officers asking for constant updates. Over the radio, I heard Phil Brown relay a request from Dryden that he wanted to see his solicitor and to speak to Superintendent Arthur Proud, whom Dryden had apparently had some dealings with in the past and in whom he seemed to have a measure of confidence.

This was great news, as far as I was concerned, as I'd worked with Arthur in the past and had a high regard for his negotiating skills. I got on to the control room immediately, requesting his presence on the plot as quickly as possible. Once he was on site, Arthur would use the firearms team's field telephone as a secure line (set to a hardwired system and not susceptible to eavesdropping) over which to speak to Dryden.

I threaded my way back to Bob. While I'd been gone, the inspectors from the management course had arrived and Bob had imaginatively used them to form an unarmed cordon at about 150 yards from the caravan, keeping away any intrepid press men or interfering rubberneckers. I cursed myself — I'd forgotten all about the inspectors and turned to see them spreading out in the field further behind us, using all the cover available. This was going to the best lesson they'd ever have in managing a firearms operation.

By this time, Phil and Andy had persuaded Dryden to accept the field telephone, which John Taylor — always a man to lead from the front — decided that he would take over to the caravan. He would be covered by Chris Barber, a tall man of few words who, although relatively new to the team, was turning out to be one of the best tactical officers they'd ever trained and in whom John had complete confidence.

Chris picked up one of the heavy Kevlar shields as if it was a bag of feathers and adjusted the strap on his MP5. Meanwhile, John tied the field telephone's wire around his belt, so he could pay it out behind him, and tucked the handset inside his ballistic vest. Then, just as they were preparing to go over the wall, Phil Brown broke radio silence to tell them that Dryden had just mentioned that he had some hand grenades in the caravan.

Events suddenly slowed to a crawl. Each man stationed

in front of the caravan and on the containment around it realised that, if Dryden reached inside the caravan where his hands couldn't be seen, there was a high likelihood that he'd be shot. It suddenly became clear to each officer there that it might fall to them to shoot Dryden at any moment and that, if that was their responsibility, it would have to be a killing shot. The two snipers slid their safety catches forward and waited.

John and Chris told me that they'd be going ahead with the plan and belly-crawled over the wall and into the field. John drew his CZ pistol, a round already in the breech, while Chris, the taller of the two men, used the Kevlar shield to protect both him and John, resting the muzzle of his carbine in the shield's carved notch. They then began to move steadily along the fence line towards the ARV men. As they passed Andy Reay, they exchanged taut grins, then kept low as they got level with Dryden, who by now was standing outside the caravan. They couldn't see any evidence of a firearm or, thankfully, any hand grenades.

They'd already agreed to try to get Dryden to come to them and take the telephone, and to this end John hailed him in his usual direct manner: 'Come and take this telephone, will you?'

'Leave it where it is,' replied Dryden.

John called out again, 'I need to explain how it works. It's not just an ordinary telephone.' Then he put the safety down on his pistol and holstered it.

Dryden's interest had been aroused and he moved over

to the fence, directly opposite John, who stood up, and leaned forward as John began to show him how to use the handset. He was just an arm's length away from John, and instinct took over. The firearms officer saw his advantage and grabbed hold of Dryden's upper body, squeezing his arms tightly by his sides. 'It seemed to be a good idea, then, just to grab him,' he later confessed.

When John made his move, Chris dropped his shield and jumped over the fence to grab hold of Dryden's wrists, handcuffing his hands behind his back. At this point, the man seemed to go limp, all resistance gone. He turned his rheumy blue eyes up at John. 'That,' he said, 'was a dirty trick.'

When he saw the cuffs go on Dryden's wrists, Phil Brown slumped, feeling suddenly exhausted as he automatically holstered his revolver and fastened the retaining clip. He then went over to help Taylor and the others, but, as he climbed over the barbed-wire fence, he winced as he caught his finger on the topmost strand, splitting the skin. He looked at his hand, blood streaming out of the cut, and thought that he could have quite easily spilled someone else's blood that day.

'You might have to use that before the end of the day.' Dryden's words.

Then he remembered how hot and uncomfortable he was and ripped at the Velcro fastenings of his suffocating body armour, hurled the Kevlar on to the ground and drew in a lungful of clean, fresh air.

ELEVEN

By the time John had made his decision to grab Dryden, the operation at the far end of Eliza Lane had grown rapidly. The mobile police station, comprising a detachable lorry trailer, had arrived at the site and I was inside, just beginning to brief Arthur Proud and Chief Superintendent Alan Miller on the situation. As I was doing so, my radio sparked into life and an unidentified voice shouted, 'They've got him! They've got him!'

I ran out into the lane and saw, over by the caravan's front door, a clutch of figures, in the middle of which was a dishevelled man with a long beard. Like ripples in a pond, the news spread that the police operation had suddenly been concluded only two and a half hours after the attempt to demolish Dryden's bungalow had begun.

Once he'd been restrained and searched, Albert Dryden

was marched along the boundary of his smallholding and into Eliza Lane, where two CID officers who had arrived with Arthur Proud drove forward and got out of their car to take Dryden from John Taylor, then bundled the gunman into the back seat while one got in beside him. Dryden's eyes darted from side to side like those of a cornered rat, as the car door slammed shut and he was whisked away to Consett Police Station.

The suddenness with which events had been concluded left me with no further plans to make. From being the venue of a volatile siege situation involving potential loss of life, the site at Butsfield had become just another crime scene.

At this point, all responsibility for the case reverted to Chief Superintendent Miller, who took over briskly and, indeed, expertly, organising resources with considerable skill. He instructed the firearms team to stay and perform a thorough search of the caravan and outbuildings, and once the weapons had been made safe and locked in the van, with an armed guard posted outside, arrangements were made for a systematic exploration of the site.

I called the inspectors back to help with the search, but no sooner had they entered the buildings than they were stopped. It appeared that, when he'd arrived at Consett Police Station, Dryden had told a CID officer that he'd planted booby-traps around the buildings on his land. Although this claim was unlikely, given the unstable nature of the man, we couldn't take any chances and all police personnel, including the firearms team, were ordered back to the junction of Eliza Lane and the A68 and a request for assistance went out to the Explosives Ordnance Depot at Catterick Garrison.

This delay meant that Harry Collinson's body had to lie where it was, alone and uncared for, and it severely hampered the police investigation and frustrated those in charge, but Dryden's warnings couldn't be ignored. Indeed, it appeared that Dryden had given further information as to the exact nature of the booby-traps, which were apparently Second World War land mines. When questioned further, Dryden had given specific details about the munitions, including the amount of pressure required to set them off, which the EOD officer admitted was accurate. The threat therefore had to be taken at face value, and the Army were tasked with searching Dryden's property, a task that was eventually concluded late that afternoon.

Meanwhile, Assistant Chief Constable Eddie Marchant had arrived in his chauffeur-driven car to see for himself what was going on. He approached Alan Miller, an old and close friend with whom he'd worked his way up through the ranks, who briefed him on events to date, and the two men then examined the site from a distance. Murders always prompted a visit by a member of the Executive Office, but Marchant quickly realised that this particular murder would receive an unprecedented level of media coverage. After all, how often do you get a murder photographed and filmed by the press?

Indeed, as Marchant looked on to the scene at Butsfield,

he heard the whirr of rotors in the air and looked up to see a helicopter hovering over the scene. He immediately rushed over to the operations centre and demanded an immediate air-exclusion order for the area, while at the same time ordering a press embargo on the transmission of images of the actual shooting and made arrangements for the seizure of the BBC film footage, on the grounds that its exposure to the public might have an effect on future judicial proceedings. Just too late, as it turned out; it hit the lunchtime news and was immediately syndicated around the world.

That was just about the extent of damage limitation for the minute. The next step was to take control of what had the potential to become a pretty ugly mess. The firearms team had officially been stood down, but they had been ordered back to the police office by Chief Superintendent Miller in order to give their statements about the incident.

Meanwhile, once the search of Butsfield was under way (before it was curtailed by the explosives scare), Bob and I drove to Dryden's home to perform a preliminary search for weapons. The information we'd received from Consett indicated that most would be at the rear of the house, in a wooden shed. We pulled up outside 26 Priestman Avenue – an unremarkable, unprepossessing 1950s semi-detached council house – and made our way around the side of building and into the back garden, where we found a garage and a shed.

As I walked towards the shed, I saw what looked like a

146

piece of drainpipe leaning against the wall of the garage. On second glance, though, it was no ordinary piece of drainpipe; it had a flat metal plate at the bottom, and halfway up there was a carrying handle that had been welded on to the pipe at an angle of sixty degrees. It was a 3in plate mortar, for God's sake!

'Bob!' I cried. 'Come and look at this!'

Bob hurried over, and when he saw what I was leaning over, he paled. There was no doubt what it was – and there, not far away in the long grass, was another mortar.

My mind reeled at the thought that, if this was typical of Dryden's handiwork, it was anybody's guess what we'd find next.

We opened the unlocked shed door to find a rusting, jumbled mess inside, like the workshop of a maniac armourer. Inside, we found gunpowder, bullet heads, cartridge cases, rifle barrels, pieces of trigger mechanism and wooden stocks, although we could see no complete firearms. In one corner, we found an old coffee jar full of silver grains, labelled bizarrely 'rocket propellant', which made us chuckle, but then Bob reached underneath the bench and drew out what appeared to be a live mortar shell, which quite frankly put the wind up both of us. Realising then that we didn't have the practical expertise for dealing with this particular piece of hardware, we withdrew and shut the shed door.

The rear door of the house gave way under a little pressure from Bob's shoulder, and then we were in the kitchen, which was clean, tidy and straight out of the

1950s. We didn't see anything untoward there, so we moved into the living room, and what we saw there stopped us in our tracks: more mortar bombs and a collection of shells arranged carefully on the hearth by a pair of men's checked slippers, presumably Dryden's. Very domestic. For all we knew, the munitions were live; neither of us was prepared to chance anything connected with Dryden.

We left the way we'd come and returned to the car, where we radioed through to Chief Superintendent Miller, who told us to take no further action until the premises at Butsfield had been checked out by the Army, who were there now. In the meantime, he said, he'd send a couple of uniformed officers over to the house to stand guard until the Army could check the place over. So Bob and I waited in the sunshine, slowly becoming aware of the neighbours' twitching curtains, as their curiosity was aroused. What had that mad farmer been up to now? They could never have guessed.

We were just about to pack up and go back to headquarters when the radio squawked again and an operator instructed us to go back to the site at Butsfield.

When we got there, the place was a hive of activity. Eliza Lane was swarming with people, all of whom were there to help build a case against Albert Dryden. The Home Office pathologist had examined the body by now, and it had been taken away for post-mortem, although the murder weapon was still in the caravan and had to be retrieved, made safe and entered in the exhibits log. Bob volunteered to go in and get it and found it exactly where Bill Lister had seen it, on a shelf by the window. It had been reloaded and contained six live rounds. Had Dryden been ready to give up without a fight, or had he been prepared to stick it out to the bitter end? We had no idea.

That was virtually the end of the operation, as far as we were concerned. We went back to Consett Police Station to meet up with the rest of the team. When we got there, we were struck by how subdued the atmosphere was, so different from the normal, vibrant thrum of well-meaning but robust banter.

Then John Taylor took Bob and me to one side and told us the news. Since the firearms team had returned to Consett nick and information about the day's events had begun to circulate, it looked as though there'd been an almighty cock-up. They'd all seen the extensive and explicit coverage on the lunchtime news, and it had affected the team badly. After all, it had been a pre-planned operation, and the ARV had been part of that plan. The problem was, if a situation involved the potential use of firearms, it was standard procedure to call out one of the tactical advisers. Nothing appeared to have been done about that, and there was certainly no mention of firearms in the operational order, a copy of which John had obtained. And if there was no intelligence of firearms, why were the ARV and paramedic on standby? Predictably, rumours sprang up around the station about the incident, about what had and hadn't been planned as the anticipated outcome.

Meanwhile, Sergeant Colin Campbell, who'd been there during the shooting, drifted in and out of the bar in which the firearms officers were waiting. Some of them tried to engage him in conversation, but he clearly had been severely traumatised by the day's events. He should have been sent home, but he'd been told to stay until he'd had a chance to be interviewed. And so he sat alone, chin cupped in his hands, gazing vacantly into space until someone came to fetch him.

The firearms team hung around in the bar until they were finally stood down at about 4.30pm, when they climbed wearily back into their van with that mortal tiredness that always follows an adrenalin rush and went back to Durham Police headquarters. Seemingly as normal, they carried their gear to the armoury, cleaned their unused weapons and put them back on the racks, a ritual of discipline instilled over the years. Eventually, they began to drift away. There wasn't a great deal of conversation.

Meanwhile, Bob locked up the armoury and set the alarm, and then he, John and I trudged up to our offices on the third floor of the nearby training block. The offices were mainly empty — the nine-to-fivers had long gone home — but a light still burned in my office, which I shared with our boss, Inspector Bill Lippett, who had been waiting anxiously for our return, hoping to get to the truth behind the rumours that had been circulating for most of the day.

As we walked into the office of the anonymously named Support Services Department, Bill must have seen the

Top: The two adversaries as young men. From his youth onwards Harry Collinson (left) was a diligent, hard worker, while Albert Dryden (*right*) was obsessed with firearms from an early age.

Bottom: The two men on the day Albert Dryden murdered Harry Collinson in front of ocals and the media.

Albert's obsession with American cars led him to make some truly eccentric
modifications (*top*). His handiwork extended to the building of a bungalow below
ground level (*bottom*). This was the final straw for the council, who had previously
been lenient about the contruction of other unpermitted buildings on Dryden's site.

Pictures courtesy of *The Northern Echo*

Top: Along with other tools and materials, Dryden's bullet making equipment enabled him to build a secret arsenal of lethal weapons that were only discovered after the killing.

Bottom: Police were astonished to discover a home-made 7.62mm firearm as well as a 3 inch plate mortar (*inset*) in Dryden's possession.

Top: 'Now I don't want any trouble Albert.' Sergeant Colin Campbell talks to Dryden at the gate with PC Steven Campbell in the background.

Bottom: Dryden warns Harry Collinson, 'You might not be around to see the outcome of this disaster.'

he final moments. In an almost trance-like state Dryden strode toward the fence, :epared to fire and discharged a fatal bullet into Harry Collinson.

Pictures courtesy of *The Northern Echo*

Top left: Reloading in Eliza Lane before going on the rampage.

Top right: Along with many others, a police constable flees the scene.

Bottom: Friends tried to dissuade Dryden from his actions, but to no avail.

Pictures courtesy of *The Northern Ec*

ryden gives a wave to his supporters as he arrives at court.

Top: It should never have happened. Harry Collinson, dead, in a ditch.

Bottom: Harry Collinson's mother, Mabel, stands at the plaque marking the nature reserve named after her son.

Pictures courtesy of *The Northern Ec*

disquiet in our faces. Although well after finishing time, the day wasn't over yet and he suggested that we all go and get a drink. And so it was that John, Bob, Bill and I ended up in the Framwellgate Moor pub the Tap and Spile, the closest decent drinking establishment to police headquarters. It was the right move, as we all seemed to need to unload, and the conversation, though stilted, revolved around our incredulity at the whole operation and our amazement at the hoard of weaponry that Dryden had accumulated. Although any criticism of individuals remained unspoken, it was clear that all three of us firearms officers had our own opinions about what should have happened. After just one slow drink, we left for our respective homes.

Elsewhere, Superintendent Ned Lawson, the deputy commander for the north division, was peeved. Distinctly peeved. He was stuck at a desk at Consett Police Station with little to do. As soon as the incident at Butsfield had broken, he'd left his office at Chester-le-Street and raced down to Consett to set up a comprehensive command system consisting of three levels: bronze, signifying on-the-ground command (carried out by Stan Hegarty); silver, which he saw as his function, operating strategically from Consett; and gold, which involved maintaining an overview of events from headquarters.

By the time he'd reached Consett, Ned found to his irritation that he'd been cut out of the loop and that matters were being dealt with directly from the force control room. Why had he been sidelined, left behind to mop up at Consett, in favour of a chief super who'd admittedly been at Durham HQ when the incident had begun? With a sense of resigned injustice, he decided to take over responsibility for communicating with relatives of the dead and injured, the council and the press.

Indeed, by this time, Consett nick was under siege from reporters for newspapers, television and radio. Ned was aware that he needed to appear firm yet co-operative until a definite account of events was available, so he was cautious when he quizzed the council's chief executive in order to glean some information about Harry Collinson's relatives. (It was imperative that arrangements were put in hand to inform Mr and Mrs Collinson straight away, especially considering the possibility of the shooting being covered on the lunchtime news.) He then contacted Northumbria Police and asked them to send a car for Harry's brother, Roy, and bring him to Consett Police Station.

After fielding some calls, speaking to both Tony Belmont's and Steven Campbell's relatives, Ned visited Shotley Bridge Hospital, where the people who'd been wounded at Butsfield had been taken, and to be honest it was a relief for him to get out of the office for a while. Ned was essentially a career CID officer who'd reached a management stage in his career, which had pulled him away from field work. He was one of the few senior ranking officers in Durham with a practical background in firearms, having served in Special Branch and the Central

Drugs Intelligence Unit at New Scotland Yard. He'd become well used to carrying a weapon as part of his job and had a unique understanding of the pressures and requirements that that entailed, being seen by many in the force as one of the most switched-on senior officers they'd ever dealt with.

When he got to the hospital, Ned half-expected to see panic and blood everywhere, but to his surprise everything was calm and orderly, as if treating patients with gunshot wounds was an everyday occurrence. As he walked into Casualty, the first person he came across was Phil Brown, who was having some stitches put in his split finger (actually a superficial wound) and who gave Ned his first eyewitness account of events. He left Phil with Andy Reay, after instructing them to head back to the station when they were finished at the hospital, as doubtless the officer investigating the events of that morning would need to see them.

Upon enquiring at the reception, Ned was surprised to find out that Tony Belmont had already left the hospital, having had the bullet removed from his arm. Aware of how essential it was to get to witnesses like Belmont as soon as possible, in order to gain maximum value from an early recall of the incident, Ned resolved to get a statement from him as soon as possible.

Eventually Ned found Steve Campbell, who was on something of a relief high, feeling lucky enough not to have lost his life. Ned had already spoken to the doctor who'd removed the bullet from Campbell's back, who had informed him that, if the path of the bullet had strayed half an inch to the right, it would have hit Campbell's spine, paralysing him for life. Fortunately, the young PC didn't seem to be aware of his close shave. Indeed, Ned noted how remarkably composed he was, considering the circumstances.

On his return to Consett Police Station, Ned went up to the bar to talk to the firearms team, whereupon John Taylor discreetly expressed his private opinions about the way things had been handled, confessing that his team had been unsettled by the rumours racing around the station by this time.

'That's really when all the trouble and acrimony started,' Ned later remembered, 'because there were all sorts of allegations and counter-allegations flying about that I knew nothing about. The main question seemed to be that, if senior police officers didn't think there was any danger from Dryden, in respect of firearms, why were armed officers on standby? Which they were, but I knew nothing about it.'

Soon, Consett Police Station was a hotbed of gossip and speculation, and the climate there that night was unpredictable. Ned knew that a firm hand was needed to keep matters under control and realised that he'd be kept busy at Consett for some time yet. Policemen are taught to be suspicious and ask questions, and Ned knew enough about firearms operations to think that, in this case, some valid questions were being raised which deserved to be answered at some stage.

Within any small community, any violent incident assumes massive proportions, but an incident of this magnitude was right off the scale, and Ned was starting to get very concerned about how Stan Hegarty, the local superintendent and a man well known and liked in the area, was dealing with events. Ned found him sitting at his desk, obviously severely affected and not functioning like the man that Ned knew, and resolved to protect him to the best of his ability. To this end, he suggested that Stan keep a very low profile for a while, as the incident at Butsfield had stirred up public feeling. Indeed, the switchboard was jammed with people trying to find out more about what had happened. He advised Stan to keep away from the press, offering to deal with them himself until the full facts were known and a proper press statement could be issued.

Stan readily agreed to Ned's proposal, and also to his suggestion that he attend the local magistrates' court in Stan's place the next day to ask for Dryden's remand in custody.

While Stan was trying to frame his thanks, Ned explained that it was perfectly understandable to be re-examining the way he'd handled things, questioning his actions, and told Stan that it was a perfectly natural reaction to have some misgivings. Yes, there would be questions asked at the inquiry – and there *would* be an inquiry. For instance, had the information and the intelligence been properly handled? Had sufficient attention been paid to Dryden's character? Had the strategic planning been correct? And had the firearms team been brought in at the right time?

Because of the fact that a man had been shot and killed, all of these considerations would be dissected and analysed and any shortcomings would be laid at the doors of the senior officers involved. Ned sympathised with Stan's position – after all, such an inquisition could befall any senior police officer – but he was nonetheless glad not to be in Stan's shoes at that time.

In fact, the forthcoming inquiry didn't seem to register with Stan Hegarty right then. Even so, Ned wanted to console him, but found that he didn't know what to say. He'd learned how to handle such situation at Police College, how to manage his men, but the skills he'd picked up there didn't seem sufficient in the face of Stan's bewilderment. And so, falling back on the only thing from his long CID experience that he could think of for a time like this, Ned took out a bottle of whisky from his briefcase.

TWELVE

Of course, it wasn't just within the police force that the effects of that day's events were felt and, by lunchtime, news coverage of the incident was being broadcast around the world. There were people in Australia who had heard of the tragedy before some of the families of those most affected had an inkling of what had happened.

That morning, Roy Collinson had been out early, getting his cattle out on to his pasture land, enjoying the warm summer sun on his back. Then, just after ten, his wife came out to find him in the barn. Wearing a concerned frown, she told him that she'd just had a phone call from a relative informing her about a shooting that had apparently taken place in Consett. All the relative seemed to know was that one person was dead and two people had been injured, and that it had had something to do with the council. It also appeared that Harry had been involved but, from the limited information available on the news, he hadn't thought that their relative was amongst the injured.

Despite the sun's warmth, Roy's skin turned cold. He wasn't as convinced about his brother's safety. Some sibling instinct told him that there was something very, very wrong, and he suddenly had the idea that his younger brother was dead.

'It's that bloody house,' he said. 'I bet it's that flaming house that they've been on about today.'

Over the preceding months, Harry had regaled Roy and the rest of their family with the saga about the eccentric Albert Dryden and the bungalow he was trying so desperately to hold on to. As well as these essentially light-hearted reports, however, Roy had had several conversations with Harry about the circumstances of the dispute and was aware that his brother was seriously concerned about the man. On these occasions, aware of his brother's attitude towards his job, and of just how stubborn he could be (a family trait), Roy had expressed his concerns to Harry and warned him to be careful. And now this mysterious phone call from a relative. Please, God, that his warnings hadn't been borne out and that Harry was alive and well!

Roy went back into the house and tried to ring Harry at his office, but found that he couldn't even get through to the council switchboard – the line was constantly engaged, mostly by relatives of other council employees seeking news of their loved ones. Those who did eventually get through were reassured, but it's ironic that the one person who was really affected couldn't get connected.

Roy was just about to redial yet again when he heard the sound of a car approaching in the lane outside. He looked out and saw a police car pulling up outside his front door. This did not bode well. Not well at all.

Roy slammed down the phone and dashed out of the back door and around the side of the house just as the startled policeman was about to knock on the door. In Roy's eyes, the officer looked barely out of nappies, fresh-faced, but his face bore a serious expression and, on seeing it, Roy's heart sank. By now, there was no doubt in his mind that his brother was dead, and all he wanted from this young man was to have it confirmed and for him to tell Roy what he should do next.

First of all, though, the policeman asked Roy formally if he could identify himself. *Identify himself?* What a stupid thing to say! All the officer had to do was ask him if he was Roy Collinson. Who the hell else was he expecting? Roy obliged, however, and then immediately asked what had happened. Never one to beat about the bush, if there was bad news, he wanted to know about it straight away.

The young man – Roy could hardly take him seriously, so self-important did he seem – asked if Roy would ring Consett Police Station, as the police there wanted to talk to him. When Roy asked him again what had happened, though, the officer replied that he'd only been asked to pass on a message from the neighbouring police force and that he really couldn't tell Roy any more.

Exasperated, and sensing that the lad knew more than he was letting on, Roy exploded. 'Well, I know fine well what it's about,' he growled and went back inside, closing the door and leaving the sheepish-looking policeman standing on his front doorstep.

Picking up the telephone directory, Roy pressed his fingers against his eyes, feeling moisture there, and looked up the number for Consett Police. To his surprise, he was connected almost immediately and, with a sour, sick feeling deep in the pit of his stomach, he heard a morose voice at the other end of the line answer, 'Consett Police.'

'Some bobby's come to my house and asked me to ring you,' said Roy. 'My name's Roy Collinson.'

Instantly, the officer on the other end of the line began to splutter and babble when he realised who he was speaking to, finally managing to explain that he'd put Roy through to another officer.

By this time, though, Roy had had enough. Firmly, he told the man on the other end of the line that he knew the matter concerned his brother and demanded that he tell him the news.

Perplexed, the officer said that he had some bad news for Roy and asked him if he was prepared for it. Frustrated, Roy told him to get on with it and after a few moments the policeman – now with some semblance of composure – said, 'I'm afraid your brother has been shot.'

Shot? Shot wounded or shot dead?

'Is he alive?'

'No. I'm afraid that he died at the scene.'

There was a pause, a heartbeat, and then the news hit Roy. That was it, then. Harry was dead, snuffed out like a candle. Memories of his brother crashed into his mind.

Then the voice on the other end of the line broke through the fog of Roy's thoughts. The policeman was offering to send a car over to Stocksfield to pick him up.

Curtly, Roy replied, 'Don't bother. I'll come myself.' He had things to do. He was the head of his family, and the others had to be told as soon as possible, as he didn't want his mother, Harry's children or his brother to hear the news from some similarly embarrassed policeman.

Meanwhile, Roy's wife was standing by the kitchen door, looking at him ashen-faced, so he called her over, sat her down and then called his children, Lisa and John. There wasn't much information at the moment, he told them, but it had been confirmed that Uncle Harry had been killed.

The questions began immediately, but he hushed them, emphasising that that was all he knew. There was an air of disbelief in the house at Stocksfield; this had to be happening to some other family.

Before Roy left for Consett, he asked Lisa and John to go over to Wolsingham to give the news to Harry's brother, Frank, who lived on a farm there high above the reservoir at Tunstall. Of course they would.

Lisa and John made their way over to Frank's isolated

farm, hardly speaking to each other during the drive. Uncle Frank was out working on the tops when they got there, gathering in his sheep, and saw their car's approach long before they saw him. He got down to the farmhouse just as they were racing up the lane.

Immediately, Frank knew that something was wrong. Had something happened on Roy's farm? Had his brother been kicked by a cow? It had happened before. Or, worse, was something up with their mother? But then his niece and nephew were getting out of the car and he could see the tears etched on Lisa's face.

'Harry's been shot!' John blurted. 'They'd gone to pull down the house of this stupid bugger at Butsfield. He started spraying about with a bloody machine gun and Harry's got shot. He's dead!'

Frank sagged, stunned at the news, and took them into the house, where John and Lisa repeated their awful message and told him of their father's dealings with Consett Police Station. They told Frank he should tell their grandmother.

Wordlessly, Frank got the keys to his Land Rover and left the house, looking neither left nor right. His wife, Ann, having never seen her husband in such a state, determined that she would go with him and just managed to climb into the vehicle and fling herself into the passenger seat as Frank gunned the engine to life. The house had been left unlocked, but what did that matter? As they drove into town, Lisa and John followed them, struggling to keep up as Frank flung the Land Rover around the sharp bends of the rutted road that led down to Wolsingham.

Mabel Collinson was in her seventies, but she still had her health and strength. She lived in a terraced cottage in the centre of the pretty Durham town of Wolsingham and was a private person, often seen tending her large vegetable garden. Every Sunday she would go to church dressed in her trademark navy-blue coat and hat, as neat as a new pin. She was devoted to her family and had a particular soft spot for her youngest, Harry, who often did odd jobs for her at her cottage, occasionally exchanging a few words with her next-door neighbours, a young couple with three children. Their name was Blackie. The husband was a policeman, apparently.

A Land Rover slewed to a halt in the lane and Frank leaped out, hurried up to the cottage's always unlocked front door and went straight in. Mabel Collinson turned at the sound of the door opening and smiled as she saw her son and daughter-in-law. What a nice surprise! They didn't usually come down from the farm during the day. She began to offer them a cup of tea, but her words hung frozen on her lips as she saw their faces.

Ann took her hand and led her to the sofa. Frank sat opposite her, wringing his big, chapped hands, not knowing how to proceed. He was a farmer and was used to direct speaking, no shilly-shallying, and so he looked at his mother, steeled himself and said simply, 'Harry's dead.'

Mabel fought for breath, her eyes locked with Frank's.

No. No, it couldn't be true. Why, Harry had visited her just that weekend. He'd sat in the same chair that Frank was sitting in now. No, it had to be a mistake. Someone else — it must have been someone else. For God's sake, children weren't meant to die before their parents!

At first, Mabel seemed to shrivel before Frank's eyes, but then she fired a fusillade of questions. Of course, Frank had little to tell her, so he told Ann to stay with Mabel while he went to find Roy and quiz him further.

As he closed the front door behind him, Frank felt a guilty relief — relief at being out of the cottage and guilt at not being able to comfort his mother. And then he realised that he had no idea where Roy was. John had said that his dad had gone to Consett, but Frank reckoned that he should be back by now and so drove over to Stocksfield. By this time, he was operating on automatic and to this day he has little recollection of the journey.

When he got to Roy's farm, his sister-in-law told Frank that his brother was still at the police station, so Frank was forced to wait for his return. He sat on the sofa and watched in disbelief as the images of his brother's death played on the television screen. It seemed almost unreal, like a scene from a TV cop show. Harry was an educated, articulate, professional man; this couldn't have happened to him. This was *Durham*, for God's sake, not the Wild West. Frank half-expected to see his youngest brother walk through the doorway, that it had all been one enormous hoax. But it wasn't. His brother was dead and the proof was right in front of him.

164

Roy eventually returned at around three o'clock, full of hell. He'd gone to the police station to find answers, but all he'd discovered there was confusion and ignorance. Nobody seemed to know what had happened or, more importantly, *why* it had happened. This man, this Albert Dryden, had been arrested and was being held at the police station, and Roy was livid, angrier than Frank had ever seen him before — angry at the man who had killed his brother, angry at the police for letting such a thing happen, angry at the council for putting Harry in danger in the first place, but most of all angry at his stupid, principled, clever, professional, stubborn and beloved little brother, who he'd now never see again.

Neither Roy nor Frank was able to comprehend the day's events. They sat and talked, trying in vain to console each other and make sense of it all.

Later that evening, when Harry's body had been moved to the local mortuary at Shotley Bridge Hospital, Roy and Frank were called down to identify him formally. In the ante-room outside, they fretted together. Time seemed to drag. Just how injured was Harry, if it was taking them this long to tidy him up? Eventually, the coroner's officer called them in and led them over to a trolley, where Harry's body lay under a white sheet. When the sheet was pulled back, they saw that Harry looked peaceful and calm. The only indication of violence was the small bluish mark on his chin where a bullet had struck. It *was* their brother — no doubt about that — but all substance had left his body. It wasn't the Harry they'd known in life, just an empty shell.

Roy formally identified Harry's body – 'That's him; that's Harry' – but Frank couldn't speak. He was numb, the cold of the mortuary was seeping into his bones and the smell of the place was overpowering, giving the air a corrupt antiseptic tang that he would never forget. And then it was time to leave their brother, alone there in the mortuary, so quiet, so cold and so alone. It just wasn't fair. He didn't deserve this. No one deserved this.

After leaving the hospital, Frank and Roy descended on Consett Police Station like a lynch mob looking for retribution, and Ned Lawson had the unenviable task of speaking to them both. Amongst their many questions, the two brothers demanded to know if the police had been aware that Dryden was armed and whether or not they'd handled the situation correctly.

Ned didn't feel able to answer that question honestly, so he said nothing. This incensed the brothers even further, and they fully vented their spleen on him, then left, muttering darkly of incompetence and cover-ups, before driving back to Wolsingham – silently, too exhausted for words – to comfort their mother.

In contrast to the Collinsons, the Dryden family seemed to deal with that day's events with a remarkable equanimity. They displayed little surprise at the outcome of the day's events, almost as if they'd known what Albert had been capable of.

Simon Donnelly, Dryden's nephew, who had been at Butsfield that day, had come across Collinson a few times while working on various building jobs but had had no direct contact with him, having been put off by Dryden's grim-faced sullenness. It was only Dryden's constant talk of how the council wanted to knock down his bungalow that coloured any view Simon had of him.

He knew that at one stage his uncle and Harry Collinson had got on tolerably well but that this relationship had deteriorated as the planning wrangle had rumbled on. He understood that Dryden had built the bungalow without planning permission, but, with it situated where it was, hidden from view, he wondered how much harm it was really doing. So, while Simon didn't have any particular liking for Collinson, he didn't think that the fellow deserved to be murdered over something as stupid as a planning dispute.

On the night before the shooting, Simon had received a call from his uncle, who asked if he would be coming up to the site the next morning. Reluctantly, Simon had agreed, but now he fervently wished he'd found an excuse not to be there. Like everyone else, when Dryden had walked out of his caravan wearing his gun belt, Simon had wanted to believe that it was a bluff, and just like everyone else, when Dryden had started shooting, he'd run for his life. Not that he believed that his uncle intended to harm him, but bullets were flying all over the place and Uncle Albert was in no state to listen to anyone, not even a relative.

Directly after the shooting, Simon had left Butsfield with his cargo of frightened council workers, whom he dropped in Consett town centre. Then, after some careful thought, he drove to his parents' house, deciding that it was best that they found out from him what Uncle Albert had done.

When Simon got to the house, his father, Peter, was ill in bed, asleep, but when he called out his mother came downstairs. Elsie had a small part-time job in a wool shop in the centre of town and, always fastidious in her dress, when Simon arrived she was getting ready to go to work.

As Elsie walked down the stairs, she could see that her son was visibly agitated. Of course, she'd known about her brother's intended showdown with the council that morning, and that Simon had gone up there. Had Albert made a fool of himself and been arrested? She knew how hot-headed he could be at times, and that he too often let his tongue run away with him. Hopefully, there would be nothing about the incident in the newspapers the next day, but she was afraid there would be, giving more ammunition to the gossips. She sat down in a chair, smoothed her skirt over her knees and waited for her son to speak.

As Simon told his mother what had occurred that morning, in brief and brutally graphic terms, she listened with mounting amazement, and when he'd finished Elsie sat silently for a long while as Simon watched for a reaction. Then she seemed to pull herself together and, with a fatalistic shrug, said, 'What's done is done. I'm going to work.'

Simon was accustomed to his mother dealing with

things in her own way – she was a very private person, not given to demonstrative displays of emotion – and could only guess at the turmoil going on beneath her calm, composed exterior. He took his cue, though, and he stood up – and then he noticed that he was still wearing his work belt. He never normally wore it in his parents' house; he'd forgotten to take it off, and his mother, who would normally have given him grief for wearing it indoors, hadn't noticed. Not today. Today was different.

As he left the house, Simon considered what to do next. Like his mother, he didn't see how anything could be fixed by giving up his work, and so, although much later than usual, he started on his daily routine as a joiner, going steadily from job to job. He took some comfort in his work, as it kept him occupied.

That lunchtime, as Simon bought a paper and something to eat, the staff in the shop were watching the news coverage of the shooting. As he was being served, the girl said to him, 'There's that bastard who shot that bloke.'

'Really?' replied Simon non-committally, not wishing to draw attention to himself, and left before anyone could make the connection between him and the footage.

'I had a lot to do,' he remembered later. 'I still had to go to work. I couldn't just go home and sit and mope about.'

Indeed, working later than usual to catch up with his backlog of work (he never let his customers down if he could help it), Simon didn't get in until after eight o'clock that night, and when he did he 'got a bit of an earwigging' from his wife, whom he hadn't contacted since the shooting and had been going out of her mind. The telephone had been ringing non-stop and she was at her wits' end.

It was only when Simon sat down in his sitting room that night that the full significance of what his uncle had done really hit him. 'When you do something like that, you have to take the consequences,' he observed later. 'It is as simple as that.'

After her son's visit that morning, Elsie Donnelly was preparing to leave the house when she received a call from the girl she worked with in the wool shop, who warned Elsie about what she might find when she got there. 'There are a lot of people coming in the shop and wondering whether you're coming in,' she said.

'Oh yes, I'm coming to work,' Elsie replied firmly and replaced the handset before the girl could ask any more questions.

As she took the bus into town that day, she felt acutely aware of the looks and whispered conversations, but she held her head high. *She* had nothing to be ashamed of; *she* had done nothing wrong. As for Albert... well, that remained to be seen.

She eventually arrived at the shop, took off her coat and waited behind the counter for her first customer. She didn't have to wait long, and soon the little shop was full of people, not all of whom, Elsie was convinced, were there solely to buy wool. How many had actually come to see the sister of a murderer? Without exception, they expressed their sympathy, telling her in concerned tones how very sorry they were about the terrible tragedy that had befallen the Dryden family, but Elsie wondered what they said when they left the shop. They peppered her with questions, but Elsie, who knew so little at this time, could say little in reply.

Somehow, she got through the day, and as soon as she got home that night the telephone rang. It was a reporter, looking to interview her. Elsie politely said no and hung up.

During the course of that evening, the telephone rang many other times, and a couple of more intrepid reporters turned up at the front door, but Peter saw them off. Anyway, what could she tell them? She hardly knew any more than they did.

The thought galvanised her into action. She'd heard on the news that her brother was being held at Consett Police Station, so she called there and asked if she could visit Albert. She was told that she could come down after eight, as the investigating officer should have finished interviewing him by then.

There were reporters camped outside the police station when Elsie arrived there that evening, but she slipped past them unnoticed. She told the officer at the front desk who she was and the officer gave her a long, cold stare and asked her to take a seat while he checked to see if she could see her brother. After a muttered telephone conversation, he indicated a door on the far side of the foyer and pressed a button to unlock it, and Elsie was ushered through.

On the other side of the door was man in a suit (Elsie took him to be a plainclothes policeman), who led her through a maze of magnolia-hued corridors until she arrived at a heavy metal gate, which a uniformed officer unlocked with an enormous key, then immediately locked it again once they'd passed through. Elsie was then shown into a bare little room furnished with a table and a few chairs and boasting a small barred window. It was a chilling place.

After a few minutes, the door opened again and Albert walked in, followed by a policeman. They both sat down, Albert in the chair on the opposite side of the table and the officer on one in the corner of the room. So, it seemed that she and her brother wouldn't be allowed any privacy.

Albert looked the same as normal, but to Elsie he seemed unaware of the seriousness of his situation. He started to talk in his usual way, gabbling about the first thing that came into his head. Concerned for his welfare, she asked if they'd fed him. Yes, one of the officers was going to get him some fish and chips a bit later on. They talked about inconsequential matters for a while, and she was dumbstruck when Albert queried, 'I wonder what time they'll let me go home?' Elsie didn't know how to respond.

After talking for around fifteen minutes, their time together was over and Albert was taken back to his cell, leaving Elsie wondering when she would ever see her brother at liberty again.

Elsewhere, people heard about the shooting in different ways. Helen Winter, Harry's erstwhile colleague (now in charge of planning at Tynedale District Council), had heard the news on Radio Newcastle while driving to Hexham to meet with friends Tom Stukins and Jack Chown, both planning officers, too. She couldn't believe it, couldn't believe that something like that could happen. She'd served enforcement notices on angry recipients herself, and had been on the receiving end of swearing and name-calling as a result, but nothing like this. It was horrific. And for Harry to be dead, sweet, gentle Harry who was always so concerned about other people's welfare...

Helen's meeting with Tom and Jack was a regular thing. She'd rung Harry just the previous week and invited him along, but he'd had to decline because, he'd said, he had to deal with some enforcement proceedings, which would take up most of his day.

After hearing the bulletin, Helen somehow made it up to her office and dialled the number for Derwentside District Council with trembling fingers. She got through to someone she knew and then listened, with mounting horror, as they confirmed the news: Harry was, indeed, dead.

Tom and Jack came up to find her and took her out for a coffee. They, too, had heard the news, and the three of them sat in a shocked silence, sipping their coffee and thinking of the one of their number who was missing, painfully aware of their own fragile mortality. Planning officers didn't get shot!

Meanwhile, the news machine had been working overtime. When Mike Peckett – dazed and lucky to be alive – finally got back to the *Northern Echo*'s offices in Darlington, he was immediately an object of all-consuming interest. This was a scoop to end all scoops, news that his colleagues would die for.

Would they, though? he wondered. *Would they really?* Mike genuinely felt that he'd faced death that morning and survived; nothing else mattered.

His camera film was processed in record time and, even before the contact prints had dried, his colleagues were clambering over desks to get a look at his pictures, gasping in amazement as they looked at Mike's images of Dryden firing the revolver and of Collinson's corpse lying in the ditch, together with shots of the build-up from early that morning. No one spoke. None of Mike's peers was a veteran of global conflicts, and it was doubtful that any had seen a dead body before, let alone one murdered in anger. He envied them; it was an event that he knew would stay with him for the rest of his life.

The stark pictures Mike had taken at Butsfield that morning would fill the pages of newspapers for months to come, and Mike had taken refuge in the mechanics of their reproduction; his only concern now was whether they were in focus and looked professional. In fact, his colleagues were full of compliments for his work, and his managers later congratulated him on a job well done, but all Mike cared about was that he never, ever wanted to be in such a situation again. In fact, he was a little piqued that his employers were admonishing him for putting himself in such danger; after all, earlier that very day his editor had been quite ready to send him back to the killing zone for more pictures.

Meanwhile, at his own desk in the same building, reporter Mark Summers had begun work on a piece about the events of that day, which he planned to back up with cuttings of the previous stories he'd run on Dryden and the history of the planning dispute. As he worked, he was aware that it was more than likely that Dryden would end up charged with a capital offence, in which case, for his own sake and that of the newspaper, he'd have to take extreme care in choosing his words in order to skirt around the laws of contempt (the assistant chief constable's warning had already filtered through) while still making the best of the story. He also knew that he was a witness to the murder and might well be called upon to give evidence.

Mark hunched over his typewriter and squeezed his eyes. He had a horrible adrenalin hangover after the events of that morning, and every time one of his trembling fingers pressed a key, somehow three letters would spring up and the jumbled keys would stick fast ('It took a hell of an age to do,' he later recalled), but he persevered. As soon as the last full stop was in place, he examined his work closely, changing a word here, adding some emphasis there, until he was satisfied that it was, at last, ready to be copy-edited. He left the office, walked down the stairs and was suddenly overcome by a fit of shaking and he was forced to cling desperately to the handrail until the sensation subsided.

Once outside, Mark retired thankfully to the Red Lion pub across the road, which was full of cab drivers and journos. As he walked in, he felt like a stranger in a western saloon: all eyes seemed to swivel towards him and the hubbub of conversation fell silent. He paused – and then the buzz of chat resumed.

Everyone in the pub that night seemed to know that Mark had been at Butsfield and, when he joined a group of friends, sat down and gladly let them buy him a drink, they talked of little else. He propped himself up against the wall and quickly downed the first couple of pints. The newspaper business has traditionally had a close association with alcohol, and on that day Mark adhered closely to tradition, staying in the Red Lion until late in the evening. Finally, a little the worse for wear, he was taken back to his home in Stanley.

The next morning, he woke early, at six o'clock, and rushed out to buy copies of all the national papers, keen to see how they'd covered the story. He wasn't due to go to work that day, but there would be follow-ups and background research to do; he had to be there. First, though, he needed some time to get himself together, so he scanned the dailies from cover to cover.

As he searched, Mark reflected on how close he had been to events. 'Usually, when you do stories, you're detached from what's going on,' he later observed, 'but I'd been part of the event. I'd been there; I'd seen it all, which is quite unusual for the majority of journalists. We normally report second-hand. We speak to the people involved, the people who saw what happened. We're not involved ourselves.'

Back at Derwentside District Council offices, news of Harry's demise had not come from any direct, official channels. Instead, somebody from the offices went out to his car, switched on the radio and heard the report of the incident. He rushed back into the offices and blurted the news to everyone he could find.

The shockwave swept through the building. Was it possible? Could one of their team really have been shot? No one knew for sure.

Shortly afterwards, more information came trickling in when the council officials who'd been at Butsfield that morning started to return, bringing with them confirmation of the news. The council's chief executive was notified and instructions were issued to the front counter staff as to how they should deal with press or general enquiries about the incident, which were soon flooding in, with phone calls jamming the switchboard and enquiring throngs filling the foyer. It was little wonder that Roy Collinson had been unable to get through on the telephone.

Once it had been established that Harry had been shot and killed, the council's general business was unofficially suspended. Throughout the building, little groups of people huddled together in corridors and offices, comforting each other and trying to come to terms with what had happened. Staff at the local NALGO (National Association of Local Government Officers) offices in Newcastle immediately made arrangements to send one of its representatives – Joe Williamson, who actually lived in Derwentside and already knew many of the employees of the council – to offer what assistance he could.

When Joe reached Derwentside District Council's offices and walked inside the building, he was immediately struck by the way the shock had affected people. No one seemed to know what was expected of them, from the chief executive down to the humblest cleaner. They'd never had to deal with anything like a shooting before and were unsure about how they should feel.

Word of Harry's death had spread like wildfire through the offices, and before long it had reached the ears of Mike Bonser, who, not really knowing how to react, had wandered the hollow corridors until, despondent, he found himself outside Harry's office. The door was ajar, so he pushed it wider and went in.

It was just as though Harry had popped out for a minute. Mike looked around and saw all the things that would have been so familiar to its occupant, feeling as if he was looking at them with new eyes. He walked around the desk and sank into the chair – Harry's chair.

There, on the desk, he saw a letter from Harry to the Department of the Environment, and when he saw the word 'Butsfield' in the heading he began to read. In his letter, Harry acknowledged the Department's final decision that Dryden's appeal against the enforcement proceedings was invalid. Turning over to the page beneath, Mike found a copy of the same letter that had been addressed to Albert Dryden. It had not been signed; it had never been sent.

THIRTEEN

Arthur Proud was a career detective, favoured by his seniors, respected by his peers and admired by his juniors, and it was to him that the task of preparing the case against Albert Dryden fell.

It was an irony that Arthur had been raised only six miles away from Butsfield and that his mother had been a cleaner for Derwentside District Council for over twenty years. As a young man, he'd craved an exciting life, and on graduating from secondary school with a clutch of O-levels he'd applied and been accepted into the Durham Constabulary not long after his nineteenth birthday. After a few years of service there, his abilities had been recognised and he'd been made sergeant. Shortly thereafter, he'd returned to Derwentside, now married and with two children.

In the force, old-time constables provide a fund of knowledge for such newly promoted sergeants to draw upon, and Joe Minto was no exception in Arthur's case. Joe was a character, both at the station and in the community, and he took Arthur under his wing and gave him a guided tour of the district. Joe had his own distinct style of no-nonsense policing that involved the judicious use of a pair of gloves that he carried yet never wore.

As Joe and Arthur meandered around the streets of Consett, they stopped at the newly built YMCA building, which boasted a fine canteen and had a reputation for serving a formidable breakfast. They ordered tea, retired to a quiet, unobtrusive, Formica-topped table, and Arthur looked around. There were only about three or four other people at the rear of the room, one of whom appeared to be holding court, talking non-stop and seeming to have everyone else's attention.

The two policemen ate their breakfasts, and on their way out they drew level with the table at the back of the room. Joe Minto stopped in his tracks, and for the first time Arthur Proud was introduced to Albert Dryden. Bearded and slightly scruffy, Dryden seemed affable and made some comment about how Arthur looked too young to be a sergeant, which provoked a ripple of laughter from his fellows and even brought a smile to Joe's usually stern features. Arthur merely blushed. They then had a brief chat about the quality of food at the YMCA, which Dryden seemed to enjoy on a regular basis.

After that brief encounter, Arthur recalls that he had no

further direct dealings with Dryden until the events at Butsfield, although he remembered regularly seeing the man around the town, often carrying a shopping bag. Arthur would always exchange a few words with him, and Dryden would respond pleasantly enough.

After staying at the Derwentside sub-division for only a couple of years, having been identified as a high-flyer, Arthur was moved around the county, working mostly in CID, until he was posted back to Derwentside some five or six years later, by this time a detective inspector. On his return, he found that little had changed; when Arthur saw him walking the streets, Albert Dryden had looked exactly the same. Everyone knew who he was and everyone spoke to him. Arthur had heard the rumours about Dryden's experiments with homemade rockets and even some about his possible illicit dabbling in firearms, but there was never anything concrete and following up such rumours was a pretty low priority.

Then, in 1990, Arthur was promoted to the rank of detective chief inspector and sent to police headquarters in Durham, to head up CID operations there. His departure was counted as a sad loss by all that worked for him at Derwentside.

Not long after the move, Superintendent (as he was then) Alan Miller summoned him to his office one day. As Arthur walked into Miller's office, he noticed a file on the super's desk, realised that this was another job for him and cursed under his breath; his in-tray was already overflowing. Miller then explained that the file related to a number of allegations made by Albert Dryden to the effect that Derwentside District Council had been involved in the sale of at least one parcel of land to one of its own employees, and that Dryden was suggesting that the council was involved in corrupt practice. As both men knew, allegations of corruption in the public sector had to be taken seriously.

'It might be a good idea if you have a look into this,' Miller said to Arthur. 'You know the area pretty well, don't you?'

Unusually, Crime Operations was free of murder investigations at the time, so Arthur, designated as the investigating officer, was free to meet with Dryden formally for the very first time. He arrived at the house in Priestman Avenue, where he reintroduced himself, and Dryden had appeared to recognise him.

Despite initially appearing extremely nervous, once Dryden got going he started to hurl accusations and conspiracy theories behind the sale of the council land. Arthur noted that the fiery little fellow seemed to know what he was talking about, though, and, if only half of what he was alleging was true, the council had indeed been corrupt or, at the least, ill-advised in their dealings with him.

To back up his allegations, Dryden then produced what he claimed to be a very powerful package of documentary evidence. Certainly, the package weighed a lot, but on closer examination its real relevance or value was debatable.

For a while, it was evident that Dryden thought that

Arthur was operating on the side of the big battalions, and a hint of suspicion hung in the air, but Arthur was a patient man and, slowly, as Dryden droned on, he gained his confidence. Although daunted by the pile of papers – almost a foot high – with which Dryden had presented him, he eventually managed to put the man's accusations, information and evidence into some sort of order.

When Dryden realised that Arthur was actually listening to him and appeared to be taking him seriously, he began to relax. It was apparent that he was genuinely aggrieved over the matter with the council, who he believed had 'stitched him up'.

Dryden's complaint had related to the piece of land at The Grove near his home that he'd intended to purchase as a smallholding, but had instead been sold to an employee of the council, and as he concluded the interview Arthur had to accept that there might be a *prima facie* case of corruption for him to investigate. He therefore took a long and detailed statement from Dryden, a task that took a further three hours.

Finally, after a comprehensive and thorough investigation, Arthur was able to return to Dryden and tell him that his allegations of corruption were unfounded. Of course, this didn't sit well with Dryden and served to compound his distrust of authority, especially as by this time he had become preoccupied with the planning saga of Eliza Lane. The file on The Grove later went before the Director of Public Prosecutions, who confirmed Arthur's recommendation that there was no case to answer.

The only discussion that Arthur and Dryden had regarding Butsfield at this stage occurred when Dryden said he was getting some bother from the council. Arthur remembers advising him at the time, 'Don't get involved in fights with them. Don't be abrasive. Just do things properly.'

Dryden had thought about this and replied, 'Basically, what you're saying is to keep my cool. Keep calm.'

'Yes,' Arthur replied. 'Exactly that, Albert.'

The two men shook hands that day and parted company. They didn't meet again until after the shooting.

On that fateful Thursday morning in 1991, Chief Inspector Arthur Proud had been in his office, working his way through a pile of reports, when one of the inspectors in Consett Police Station's control called him, informing him of the shooting at Butsfield. 'As soon as they said "Butsfield",' Arthur remembers, 'I thought, "Oh no. It's got to be Albert Dryden."'

Arthur was told that the shooter was now surrounded by armed police and had asked for Arthur Proud by name, while the senior officers at the scene were also requesting his presence as a negotiator because the situation had degenerated into a stand-off.

Arthur slammed down the phone and ran down the corridor to find Inspector Tom Ryan. The pair worked as a team (negotiators never work alone) and were considered to be exceptionally good in what was a very refined area of expertise. They found a car at the pool and made straight for Butsfield.

Not far out of Durham, Tom and Arthur encountered some roadworks, governed by temporary traffic lights. Hearing sirens coming up behind him, Arthur pulled over to let the firearms team past and then followed them through the red light – which prompted a PC in the back of the van to shake his fist at them, obviously not realising he was doing so at two senior officers.

As they drove, Arthur trawled his mind for any useful nuggets of information about Dryden and recalled their last conversation, concerning Dryden's attempted land purchase. 'Keep cool,' Albert had agreed then. 'Keep calm.' He obviously hadn't taken Arthur's advice to heart.

The car journey to Butsfield seemed to take an age, and when they finally arrived at Eliza Lane Tom and Arthur were directed to the mobile police station, where I would fill them in on what had happened so far and Chief Superintendent Alan Miller would give them instructions. I'd worked with both men on previous firearms operations and had a high regard for their abilities.

Surveying the scene through the mobile station's window, Arthur noticed that an outer cordon of unarmed police officers, all wearing white shirts, had been established, as well as two figures, about twenty yards apart, by the far fence line, facing a caravan in the next field, where a man was sitting calmly on the steps. He screwed up his eyes: Dryden.

I began the briefing, informing Tom and Arthur that, in addition to the unarmed containment at a safe distance, a ring of armed officers had surrounded the caravan.

Arthur knew, then, that Dryden had placed himself in extreme danger. These boys didn't mess about, and the slightest wrong move could provide two cold corpses to finish the day. But his mood lifted when he heard that two ARV officers were in talks with Dryden. Excellent. That would make his and Tom's job a great deal easier when they took over the dialogue.

'From the information I had,' Arthur later remembered, 'they'd been talking to Albert. And they'd done a bloody good job, by all accounts.'

Lastly, I told them that John Taylor would soon be taking a secure field telephone down to Dryden, which would enable Arthur to talk to Dryden.

'Good,' thought Arthur. 'I know the man. Hopefully he'll have some confidence in me. Hopefully, they would be able to settle him down and quickly resolve the siege.'

Just as Arthur and Tom were leaving the caravan, I called them back. Suddenly, it seemed that their skills as negotiators were no longer required; the situation had been defused by John Taylor's daring arrest of Dryden. The siege was over. However, the two negotiators weren't going to get away as lightly as that, and Alan Miller put Arthur in charge of interviewing Dryden, to be assisted by Tom, who went about setting up the incident room.

By this time, the officers in the field had gathered a number of statements from eyewitnesses to the shooting (many of whom, including police officers, were now making suggestions that Dryden was mentally disturbed and that there might be explosives on the site), but now

Arthur and Tom needed to put some flesh on these bare bones. As they were doing this, Dryden was frogmarched up from his caravan and bundled into a squad car, which slowed momentarily beside Arthur before speeding away to Consett Police Station.

'Albert saw me,' Arthur recalled. 'His head was down, his chin was on his chest and his eyes were looking up at me. He just looked like a little lad who was in big trouble and didn't know what was going to happen next. He looked absolutely terrified.'

By the time Arthur had arrived back at Consett Police Station, Dryden had just been booked in, a normally quick process that had been stretched out by Dryden's pedantic nature and his desire to tell anyone within earshot the entire history of the planning dispute. He'd been told why he had been arrested and had asked for his solicitor to be informed. At this point, the duty officer would normally have retrieved all his personal belongings, including his belt and shoelaces, but, because of the seriousness of his crime, these were all retrieved and bagged by the two detectives who had brought him in. Dryden was then instructed to remove all of his clothes, item by item, and these too were all individually bagged and labelled for later forensic analysis. By the time Arthur got to him, Dryden looked scared and vulnerable in his paper boiler suit and plastic slippers as he was escorted down to the cells.

Arthur scrounged a quick cup of tea and then found an office, sat down and started to plan his first interview. He knew he had to be careful; this was a high-profile murder investigation and he didn't want to give Dryden any false hopes or put words in his mouth. He'd already made sure that someone had suggested to Dryden that it was in his best interests to be represented by a solicitor.

His preparations complete, Arthur went downstairs to the cells – familiar territory (he'd lost count of the number of prisoners he'd interviewed in this nick) – and asked for Dryden to be brought to an interview room, then stood in the charge room, watching as the prisoner was escorted through. From looking 'absolutely terrified' in the back of the squad car at Eliza Lane, by now Dryden was looking a lot tougher. He seemed to Arthur to be weighing up what was going on, as if he was working out how he could make things best for himself.

After Dryden had been in the interview room for a few seconds, Arthur walked in, looked at Dryden and muttered sadly, 'Albert. How on earth has it got to this?'

There was no response. Dryden was obviously thinking hard about what to say next.

Arthur needed some information and went on quickly, 'I've got a lot of people up there. They're my people. I don't want anybody tripping up, falling into holes, having accidents or anything like that.'

Without looking at him, Dryden asked, 'Where are they at?'

'They're all outside the area at the moment.'

'Just as well,' said Dryden, 'because I've got landmines buried.'

Arthur gaped at him in disbelief. *Landmines?* As if to reassure himself, he said, 'Ah, you haven't, man!'

But Dryden insisted that he'd planted landmines around his property and went on to describe clinically how he'd sown them into the ground in a random pattern. He gave Arthur technical specifications of the mines he'd used (which, of course, meant nothing to Arthur) and described the materials they were made from and the amount of pressure required to trigger them (39lb per square inch – approximately the weight of a goat). If he was capable of this, thought Arthur, what other secrets were lurking up at Butsfield? Dryden was evidently a man to be taken seriously – at least, until anything to the contrary could be proved.

Once he'd got over his initial astonishment, Arthur got Dryden to draw him a map of the mines' locations and told one of his officers to get it to Alan Miller immediately. Then he radioed the chief super himself, telling him of the new development and advising him to withdraw all personnel to a safe distance.

The interview had suddenly become a priority. Arthur had to find out what other secrets might be revealed, if any. It would be a long, drawn-out exercise –particularly because, by this time, Dryden's solicitor had arrived.

So the formal interview began. The whole event was tape-recorded and there were several pauses for refreshment. 'He was in survival mode,' recalled Arthur later. 'He knew he'd been caught; he knew he was knackered, in terms of what he was going to be charged with and that he'd go to Crown Court. He consulted his solicitor at length before and during the interviews. I don't think it was a case of his solicitor telling him what to say or what not to say; this was Albert in a pickle, and he had to do the best for himself.'

Meanwhile, Phil Brown and Andy Reay had returned to the police station – after Phil had been treated at the hospital – to write up their notes of the day's events. Although by now bone-tired, they set to the task, careful not to omit the slightest detail, then went down to the cell block to see Arthur, currently interviewing Dryden. Phil knocked on the door and they entered to see Arthur, Dryden and a solicitor seated around the table. Dryden no longer looked so much of a threat in his paper suit, and Phil and Andy could hardly reconcile this strange-looking creature with the maniac they'd witnessed that morning. Phil had an overwhelming urge to throttle him, then and there, for what he'd put them through.

Phil and Andy read out the notes they'd made, word by word, reliving the events of the past few hours. Then Dryden himself read laboriously through this record, his finger following every word. This took some considerable time, to the frustration of everyone else in the room, but he wouldn't be hurried; he was, once again, the focus of everybody's attention.

Dryden turned the final page, looked up and saw that all eyes were on him. OK, he was prepared to agree with the bulk of Phil and Andy's report, although he quibbled over some minor points (out of sheer bloody-mindedness, the officers present thought).

Dryden then alleged that, on his arrest, he'd been assaulted by PC Brown, whom he recognised, and Sergeant Taylor, whom he described. This brought a wry smile to the faces of the officers present, as this is the most common post-arrest complaint. And, in any case, Phil had never got close to him; he'd been impaled on the barbed-wire fence at the time. Short of waiting for him to surrender, which hadn't seemed at all likely, the officers had been forced to apprehend Dryden physically. In reality, he should have thanked his lucky stars that he hadn't been dealt with more harshly.

It was a futile argument. Dryden refused to sign the notes as a true record of what had happened – although this didn't really matter; it had at least been recorded that he'd read them.

Dryden's refusal to acknowledge the police's version of events was in fact common of many people charged or accused of an offence, especially those who know they're guilty. Frequently, the culprit sees this as a device whereby he might escape penalty by introducing a technical flaw to the evidence, whereas in reality the police and the judiciary are usually pretty wise to this ploy. Nonetheless, it was Dryden's right not to sign, and there was no need to persuade him otherwise.

The interviews were finally over by 9.50pm, following a meal break and a brief visit by Dryden's sister, Elsie. By the time Dryden was returned to his cell, the traffic men and the solicitor had gone home and Arthur was sitting exhausted at his desk, reviewing the progress they'd made and preparing things for a quick start the following morning. There was still a great deal to be done, but the main impression he'd carried away from that day's interview was that not once had Dryden shown any trace of remorse. But now, at last, he was done for the night.

The telephone rang shrilly. The custody officer from the cellblock was on the other end of the line. Apparently, Dryden wanted to speak to Arthur again, and so, exhausted and exasperated, he trudged back down the stairs. Almost before he got into the cell, however, Dryden apologised: 'Look, I'm sorry. I've been under an awful lot of pressure. I swear that I *had* mined my land up there, but I've dug them up and I took them away. I thought better of it. They're down the bottom of the shaft, up at Rookhope.'

Arthur asked Dryden if he'd be prepared to take him there the following day and point out exactly where he'd dumped the mines, and the prisoner readily agreed. Arthur then pressed Dryden, stressing that he was concerned about innocent people getting injured at Butsfield and that he'd better not be messing him about.

'No, they should be all right,' replied Dryden. 'As long as they aren't ignorant of weapons and bits of weapons, they'll be all right.'

Satisfied at last, Arthur left Dryden in his cell and went back upstairs to call Alan Miller, who was also still on duty. They agreed that the crew from the Explosive Ordnance Depot – whose numbers by now had been supplemented by another team from their Kent headquarters – would stay and continue their operations at Eliza Lane and Priestman Avenue. As a great deal of munitions had already been recovered from both locations, the visit to Rookhope wasn't a major priority and would be arranged after Dryden had been charged.

Arthur put down the phone, switched off his desk light and left the station after a long and gruelling day – in fact, the first of many such days on the case. With Dryden languishing in his cell, Arthur climbed into his car and hoped he'd be home in time to say goodnight to his children.

Almost as soon as he arrived at the station the next morning, Arthur was called down to the cellblock by the custody officer, who told him that, not long after he'd arrived on duty at 6am, Dryden had woken and pressed the buzzer in his cell – and then continued to press it, repeatedly. He had been very upset and agitated but wouldn't tell the officer why; he just kept repeating that he wanted to talk to Arthur.

At that point, there was a loud buzzing noise.

'That's him again,' muttered the sergeant impatiently. 'This has been going on non-stop for the last two hours.'

The two men then walked down to Dryden's cell. With much clanking of keys (and a look of relief), the custody officer opened the flap in the door of Dryden's cell. As he did so, there was a sound of scuttling feet and they saw the prisoner cowering over on the cell's wooden bench in terror, squeezing as far away from the door as he could get.

'Open the door,' demanded Arthur. More clanking ensued and then the heavy steel door swung open and Arthur walked into the cell. 'What's up, Albert?' he asked.

Dryden looked fearfully into the far corner of his cell. 'It's him!' he said, quailing.

Arthur followed the man's gaze and then looked back at him, not understanding.

'*It's him!*' Dryden repeated. 'There!' He pointed to the corner of his cell. 'I keep imagining Harry Collinson's there. He's in the room with me.'

Arthur was immediately suspicious. He'd seen prisoners try it on like this before, hoping to build a defence based on grounds of diminished responsibility. He told Dryden that his vision – if that's what it was – was simply an acute reaction to his circumstances and that he was imagining it. Then, brusquely – knowing that Dryden would have to be interviewed again before he could be charged – he told the prisoner, 'There's a fair bit of work to get through today.'

That seemed to bring Dryden back to reality, as he quickly forgot about his imaginary visitor. By this time, his breakfast had arrived and, as he fell hungrily on it, Arthur left him to it, going back to his office to pick up on overnight developments in the case and to prepare for the next interview. He was well aware that Dryden had already been in custody for some time and he knew that he had to either charge him later that day or release him. And the second choice, Arthur thought grimly, wasn't an option.

Back in the interview room, later that morning, Arthur switched on the tape recorder and reminded Dryden that he was still under caution. Then, once the preliminaries were out of the way and Dryden was relaxed, the chief inspector dropped a bombshell.

Arthur told Dryden that some correspondence had been found at Priestman Avenue that had obviously been delivered on the previous day, while Dryden had been at Eliza Lane. Amongst this, he said, was a letter, which he then brought out, unfolded slowly and placed on the table, smoothing it with his hands. He pushed it over to Dryden.

The letter was a formal communication from the Department of the Environment informing Dryden that his final submission for an appeal against the council's actions was groundless and that his application was therefore invalid. It was a copy of the same letter that had arrived on Harry Collinson's desk and been read by Mike Bonser.

The letter was the final nail in the coffin for Dryden. If he'd received this letter the previous day, he would have (according to his statement) begun dismantling the bungalow 'brick by brick'.

One of the enduring questions, however, is, if Dryden *had* known the contents of this letter, would it have made any difference to his actions that day? While everyone else present in the stuffy little interview room couldn't help but marvel at the poor timing of this communication, the news seemed to have no impact on Dryden, who just read the letter slowly, his face an impassive mask.

The interview then began and Arthur laboriously

worked through the detail of the previous day. Then Arthur asked Dryden a question about the gun with which he'd killed Harry Collinson, and at this point he remembered seeing Dryden's eyes light up. The question seemed to appeal to his ego, giving him an opportunity to air his knowledge of firearms.

'Well, what I used to do it was a .455 Webley revolver: a manstopper,' replied Dryden proudly. 'Manufactured between 1902 and 1907.'

It was at this fundamental point, Arthur recalled, that Albert Dryden finally admitted to the murder of Harry Collinson. His pride had taken over and he'd made a crucial slip, giving Arthur all the information he needed to prise the case wide open. Dryden had indirectly admitted to killing Harry Collinson and seriously wounding two other men.

His heart racing, Arthur tempted Dryden further down that path, using the man's vanity to lead him to his own destruction, and so Dryden duly described in detail the rounds he'd used, what they were made of and their ballistic capabilities. Dryden's enthusiasm in discussing the weapons he'd used on Arthur's own officers sent a frisson of revulsion down his spine, but at last they were finally getting down to the core of Dryden's testimony.

After the interview had been terminated, Arthur took Dryden to Rookhope, high in nearby Weardale, where the gunman identified a deep mineshaft into which he claimed he had thrown the landmines he'd planted and then dug up from his property. The explosives experts were summoned, but they were unable to find any trace of them. It was decided that they had probably been washed away by an underground stream – if, of course, they'd ever existed.

Dryden had perked up visibly during his trip out into the countryside, chatting amiably as he was deposited back in his cell. Then his expression became hooded and a black gloom descended upon him.

Before the twenty-four-hour charge-or-release limit had been reached, Arthur Proud charged Albert Dryden with the murder of Harry Collinson and two counts of attempted murder against Tony Belmont and PC Steven Campbell. Dryden was scheduled to appear before Consett Magistrates' Court two days later and was remanded into custody for a further seven days at the police station. The investigation, however, had just begun and would continue until sufficient evidence had been gathered to ensure Dryden's eventual conviction.

Collins' *Concise Dictionary* defines evidence as 'data on which to base proof or to establish truth or falsehood' – ie all the relevant information required to prove to a court of law that a defendant is guilty of the offence or offences with which he or she has been charged. And the gathering of evidence of a crime as serious as that with which Albert Dryden was charged is a mammoth task. Everyone involved, whether directly, as a bystander or as a character witness, would have to be interviewed, and some would be quizzed more than once.

For example, one of the prime unidentified witnesses being urgently sought by the police was a burly man with long blond hair who'd been standing nearby as Dryden had harangued council officials at Butsfield, and Dryden's supporters – uniformly guarded and close-mouthed when interviewed – seemed strangely unable to identify him. From the video footage retrieved after the incident, it was clear that he was wearing a workman's belt with a hammer stuck into it, draped over his thigh almost like Dryden's gun belt, but none of Dryden's cohorts seemed willing or able to identify him.

Then, two days after the shooting, two police officers revisited Dryden's sister, Elsie Donnelly, who had already proved to be an invaluable source of background information concerning Dryden's character. As they were leaving her house, almost as an afterthought one of the detectives showed Elsie a picture of this mysterious man that they wanted to interview. Of course she recognised him. It was her own son, Simon Donnelly. She gave them his address and the two detectives went straight around to see him.

As Simon was a joiner by trade, he habitually wore a thick leather belt equipped with a claw hammer, and when he opened his front door the detectives recognised him immediately from the video. He was frank and helpful, and he told them plainly what he'd seen and heard on the previous day with no attempt at prevarication. He knew that there could be no excuse for what his uncle had done, whatever the provocation; he'd witnessed the sequence of events that had led to the murder itself and gave his statement without fear or favour. Lightheartedly, he chided the detectives for not being able to trace him earlier, as during the incident his van, clearly advertising his name and phone number, had been parked at the side of the road.

So began the enormous job of putting together the evidence required for Dryden's prosecution, and Arthur Proud wanted no stone left unturned, no question unanswered. Interviews were conducted with the two injured men (both still traumatised by the affair), and all the eyewitnesses were to be traced and interviewed.

When it came time to interview the journalists who'd been present that day, some found themselves on the horns of a professional dilemma. Mark Summers, from the *Northern Echo*, for instance, recalled that he had to tread a fine line, as there could easily have been a conflict of interest between his duty to tell the police everything he knew about and saw at the incident and his role as a journalist, which was to publish his story – without breaking the rules governing the admissibility of evidence. He therefore had no alternative than to be completely open in his dealings with the police, but he'd have to wait until after the trial before he told the whole story. Of course, there was so much captured video evidence of the shooting that even Dryden's supporters found it difficult to defend his actions.

There was a great deal of physical evidence to be gathered. One of the more gruesome tasks, yet unfortunately a necessary one, was to determine the exact cause of Harry Collinson's death. The possibility that there might be explosives at the site had meant that the local Home Office pathologist, Dr Ranasingh, had been able to perform only a brief post-mortem examination of his body where it lay before it could be moved, later that day. Later, Dr Ranasingh performed a full autopsy, after which he concluded that Collinson's death had been caused by being shot once in the heart. Subsequent to his death, he had been shot once in the right lung and once in the chin.

By this stage, it had been forensically determined that the weapon and rounds that had caused these injuries were indeed a .455 Webley revolver and Dryden's homemade 'manstopper' cartridges, and, in addition to the murder weapon, the police recovered three further pistols, three rifles and two shotguns from the scene at Butsfield. The haul from Priestman Avenue, meanwhile, was even more extensive, comprising six pistols, twelve rifles, one shotgun, two homemade mortars with eight various shells, and a plethora of spare parts, cartridges, powder and live ammunition. There was also a 20mm cannon, designed by Dryden to fit on to a bracket welded on to the bonnet of one of his reconditioned vintage cars, perhaps in preparation for an assault on the council's offices. Details of this haul were soon relayed to the press, largely because Arthur Proud was aware that the police would need their full co-operation.

There was no doubt that Dryden had murdered Collinson and wounded Belmont and Campbell – all the evidence supported the charges. Two of the most telling pieces of evidence, which would in addition secure Dryden's conviction for the attempted murder of another person, were the two pieces of video footage capturing the shooting. BBC reporter Tony Belmont and his camera crew had provided the unspoken witness that would eventually prove this intent, while Harry Collinson, in his efforts to be totally up front in the council's dealings with Dryden, had set up the council's own video camera on the site, operated by a colleague.

It's interesting to note that Harry set up the council's camera for a particular purpose. What Dryden didn't know was that, if he'd obstructed the council peacefully, they would have backed off; they would have loaded the digger back on to the low-loader and driven it away. Their purpose in recording the events on video was so that they could have placed it as evidence before a High Court judge in the last stages of the enforcement proceedings – more evidence to support the suggestion that Harry had tried to resolve the confrontation as amicably as possible.

One would be forgiven for thinking that either of these pieces of video evidence would have captured Dryden actually shooting Harry Collinson, but, unfortunately for Arthur Proud, this wasn't the case. Both recordings were taken from different, entirely separate viewpoints. In the council video, taken from Eliza Lane, Dryden can't be seen at all and only Collinson's back is visible, while the BBC video shows only the view of Albert Dryden from the front and nothing of Collinson. This difference in sight lines and perspective led to a difficulty in determining the exact position of the two protagonists and witnesses at the scene and was in danger of rendering their evidential value useless.

Then Arthur struck lucky. One of the officers in the Durham Constabulary had recently transferred from the Metropolitan Police and had worked on their groundbreaking Football Intelligence Unit, which was involved in spotting offenders in large crowd situations and identifying their criminal actions from video recordings. By using his expertise, as well as that of his erstwhile colleagues in London, a world of additional information was brought to light. From him, the technical officers in Durham learned how to grid-mark the screen so that a witness could describe his exactly location, as well as that of the events he or she witnessed. They were therefore able to build up a verbal account, based on the video record, which served to clarify statements made by witnesses. This was a major breakthrough in developing the case and saved many man-hours.

Late one night, while sitting at his desk after everyone else had gone home, Arthur Proud worried at a niggling doubt that he'd overlooked something. He could understand the confrontation between Dryden and Harry Collinson, who represented the authority which Dryden so resented, and therefore there was a logical progression culminating in Collinson's murder. But why had Belmont and Campbell been shot? Where was the logic in that? How could that possibly benefit Dryden? There was something else, something he'd missed. There *had* to be.

'There are four considerations that one has never to forget as an investigating officer,' Arthur later revealed. 'What is the motive? What is the opportunity? What was the subsequent action? But first of all, what were the preparatory steps? Most of these seemed clear and self-explanatory, but why was he shooting at people who appeared to be running away? Why wasn't he shooting at people he didn't like?'

Then it came to him: Dryden *was* shooting at someone he didn't like, someone he'd already admitted while being interviewed that he wished he'd killed. But he hadn't, had he? He'd missed, and not once but twice. Dryden might not have been the crack shot he'd claimed to be.

When he returned to the station the next morning, the first thing Arthur did was ask the technical team working on the videos if it was possible to analyse the tapes any better; he needed more information. One expert mentioned a facility called underscanning. On a normal television screen, the man explained, there's a border, usually around an inch and a half wide, around the recorded transmission picture, and the viewer doesn't see what's behind this border. By using a professional underscanning facility, however, the dimensions of the footage can be shrunk so that the whole image is visible.

Arthur told the team to go about underscanning the footage they'd retrieved from the scene, and when the process was complete he watched the council tape through again. This time he could see a figure wearing a brown suit standing right next to PC Steven Campbell. He then watched the BBC tape, and, yes, there was the man in the brown suit again, this time standing next to Tony Belmont as he was shot.

Arthur knew only too well who the man in the brown suit was: Michael Dunstan, the council's solicitor and, it seemed, a very lucky man (Dryden had indicated his hatred of the man many times during the interviews). Got him! The expanded video footage finally gave Arthur the evidence he needed to charge Dryden ith an additional count of attempted murder.

FOURTEEN

The local, national and international news media had been mobilised by the shooting at Butsfield, particularly as one of their own had been injured, and, within hours of the incident, the press machine had gone into overdrive. Editors sent out investigative journalists on a hunt for background information, especially from the council and the police. The doorstepping of friends and family was considered legitimate, and reporters vied with each other to get to the people closest to both Dryden and Collinson in their search for raw, emotional copy for a hungry public.

Within hours, Roy Collinson was being pressed for his reactions on the incident, particularly on the conduct of the police and Derwentside District Council. By this time, a shell of bitterness was already starting to harden around

Roy, who was angered by the Consett Police's insensitive response to his grief, and he spoke at length to the press about how he thought the incident had been mishandled with the vehemence that only the loss of a loved one can bring. Of course, this was all grist to the news mill and would fill many column inches around the world.

Two days later, Roy received a telephone call at his home from Stan Hegarty, who invited Roy down to the station. He knew that Roy had been speaking to the press and wanted to explain the events from the police's point of view and, no doubt, to engage in some damage limitation.

Roy was affronted by Hegarty's approach. He knew the superintendent socially and was offended that he didn't seem able to make the effort to come out and see him at his home, rather than summoning him into the station. After all, he wasn't one of Hegarty's officers. However, Roy decided to shelve his anger and go and hear what Hegarty had to say.

As he sat in Hegarty's office, his temperature rose as he listened to what he felt were mealy-mouthed excuses for the police's actions, or rather the lack thereof. Hegarty's pleading explanations that the police had no intelligence indicating the possibility that Dryden might contemplate the use of firearms cut zero ice with Roy, and he challenged Hegarty on the matter. By this time, he'd found out about how, prior to the shooting, Garry Willey had warned the police that Dryden had confessed his intention to defend his property with firearms, and many people had beaten a path to his door to tell him of Dryden's reputation for eccentric behaviour and an unhealthy preoccupation with guns.

Roy left the police station that day dissatisfied and disgusted. 'I never asked for a police inquiry, as I knew it would be a waste of time,' he later said bitterly. 'It was just going to be a smoothing over. One's covering for another. It's all dovetailed in, straight away. "Why didn't you have your response team at the scene?" "Well, we didn't know he had a gun." And was it just a coincidence that the firearms team *happened* to be in the area at that time. So how can you prove otherwise? Because this is the police. They're all going to cover for each other, right away, down the line. It's a waste of time.'

It wasn't just Harry Collinson's relatives who were angry. Many in the force, too, were concerned about how the event had been planned.

On the Friday morning after the shooting, the firearms tactical advisers gathered in their office, as usual. Unlike the fairly subdued atmosphere that reigned the previous evening, however, there was a lot of very vocal consternation. The advisors spent that entire morning on a wholesale dissection of the planning, tactics and post-incident procedures that had been employed at the incident at Butsfield, and much was made of the fact that there'd been no consultation regarding what was, in effect, a pre-planned firearms incident. As the advisers saw it, an integral part of the operational order had been the ARV, the inclusion of which meant that the operation was pre-planned and therefore warranted seeking their advice before the event.

This wasn't just a case of sour grapes at not being consulted; their view was enshrined in nationally agreed guidelines. Accepting that twenty-twenty hindsight is a wonderful asset, they knew that not many superintendents would have gone against the views and recommendations of a tactical adviser, but in this case those views hadn't even been sought. Some on the team knew of several senior officers who thought of them as an essential resource, available for consultation twenty-four hours a day, and the general view was that it would be an imprudent man who wouldn't take advantage of their expertise at the merest whisper of the word 'firearm'.

One such superintedent was Ned Lawson, who remembered, 'There were times when I registered my approval of the way the tactical firearms teams were used. I know that they're an expensive resource, but expensive resources in such situations are absolutely necessary and shortcuts can't be taken.'

Later, John Taylor, the man who eventually arrested Dryden, pointed out, 'The training department knew nothing of this operation. I think we should have been consulted, at least, and asked for advice and assistance. After all, part of our role is to give tactical advice.'

That Friday morning, the firearms advisers mulled over what their recommendations for the operation might have been, had they been involved in the planning stages. They agreed that, had they been consulted, they would have suggested two options: either an early-morning raid to search for firearms, far away from the attentions of the press (there was certainly enough suspicion that Dryden was in illegal possession of weapons, even if such a suspicion was based solely on Dryden's own boasts), or the deployment of covertly armed officers at the scene – not at Consett Police Station, where they were of absolutely no use whatsoever. Had the second option been taken, they could then have cleared the crowd and challenged Dryden immediately. Had he then been stupid enough to draw his weapon and threaten to fire, he would doubtless have been shot. Either way, there would be no loss of innocent lives. The advisers unanimously agreed that their preferred choice would have been the early-morning raid, on the basis that prevention would have been better than cure.

Bill Lippett listened intently to the discussion. These were professional judgements and, as such, had to be taken seriously. Now it was a question of what to do next. He had to take the matter further, if only so that lives wouldn't be put at risk in the same way in future operations. He had a good relationship with Assistant Chief Constable Eddie Marchant and agreed to request of him an in-house debrief of the operation as soon as possible.

Bill went to see Marchant and laid out a convincing case, but his request for a debrief was refused. The reason given was that the Dryden case was now a murder inquiry. There had been little police involvement before the shooting and, if an inquiry was to be held, it should be done by the council.

When Bill returned to the office and announced his lack of success, the news was greeted with a distinctly frosty reception and dismay by his staff.

Early on Monday morning of the following week, I was first in the office, drinking my first coffee of the day and checking through my mail, when my boss, Superintendent Dick Cooksley, the Head of the Personnel and Training Department, put his head around the door to say hello. We exchanged a few words, and then Dick mentioned Bill Lippett's request for a debrief of the Dryden shooting. He pointedly warned me to be very careful, as at least one of the executive officers was apparently 'very prickly' about the whole Butsfield situation.

After he'd left the office, I just sat there, open-mouthed at the implications of Mr Cooksley's words. Why would such an obvious warning be delivered in such a way? Was there indeed something to hide about the way the operation had been planned? I was so concerned that I took the unusual step of writing down the warning verbatim in my notebook.

After some consideration, I called PC Bill Clementson, the secretary at the Durham Constabulary Federation Office, the police union. Bill had been the Durham force's Federation representative for as long as I could remember, and I didn't take my decision to call him lightly, as Bill was aware – as was just about everyone else in the force by now – of the circumstances surrounding the shooting at Butsfield. I reluctantly expressed my deep concerns about the situation, not least about the absence of a debrief, and then confessed that I was so suspicious about senior management that I didn't want to be seen discussing the matter at headquarters. Feeling almost like a spy, I asked Bill if he would be prepared to meet in the car park of a nearby pub that morning at eleven. He agreed.

Soon after, the rest of the firearms instructors arrived in the office and milled about, drinking coffee, before going about their duties. I remember being quiet and subdued, choosing not to mention my meeting with Bill, as the fewer people that knew about it, the better.

At ten to eleven, I snatched a sheaf of papers from my desk (including a copy of the operational order from the previous Thursday) and left the office, muttering about having to go into Durham to collect something, then headed down to the basement car park, got into my own car and drove out of police headquarters. Although I knew I was being paranoid, I couldn't help checking to see if anyone had noticed me leaving.

When I reached the pub car park – almost empty at that time of day – I pulled into a parking bay, switched off the engine and waited. After only a couple of minutes, Bill Clementson drew in next to me, and I got out of my car and climbed on to the passenger seat of Bill's.

'Thanks for meeting me like this, Bill,' I began, almost apologetically. 'I wasn't comfortable doing this at headquarters. Look, Bill, I'm very concerned about the way the Butsfield incident was handled.'

'So am I,' Bill replied diplomatically. 'So is everyone.'

'It was a shambles,' I went on. 'It should never have happened. They didn't consult a tactical adviser and they didn't comply with the Association of Chief Police Officers' Firearms Manual.'

That woke Bill up. 'Are you sure about this?' he said sharply.

I nodded. 'Absolutely positive. And now they're trying for some severe damage limitation. They're refusing to hold a debrief.'

Bill was amazed. 'Why not? I mean, if they've got nothing to fear...'

'Well, let's put it in context,' I said. 'I was very firmly warned off this morning from making any waves about this. That's what made me ring you.'

'Oh. Warned off, were you? Who by?'

'Superintendent Cooksley. But I think he was just the messenger. We asked Bill Lippett to request Eddie Marchant for a debrief, but all he got was a very firm no. What I'm looking for is for the Federation to take this forward and formally ask for an inquiry. They might take some notice if the request came from you.'

'OK,' said Bill reservedly.

'Here's a copy of the operational order,' I said, passing over the two-page document. 'See? It clearly shows that the ARV was on standby at Consett Police Station. If that's not a pre-planned operation, I don't know what is.'

Bill slowly read the document and handed it back. He looked thoughtful. 'You know, this should never have happened. Not like this. We've got a perfectly legitimate right to ask for an inquiry. I mean, one of our members has been seriously injured.'

Bill agreed to see what he could do as soon as he got back, and I was confident that he'd do his best. Nevertheless, I felt sick when I got back to headquarters and sat in my car for a long while before going back upstairs. An illusion died for me that day. Until that Monday, I'd always been an organisation man – totally committed to the force – and, in my (perhaps naïve) view of a disciplined service, it was fundamentally necessary to trust your superiors to do the right thing. Sure, poor decisions could be taken but, if they were made honestly, where was the shame in owning up to your mistake? That day, I felt ashamed to be a police officer.

I found myself facing an awful personal dilemma. On the one hand, I had a moral responsibility to bring the affair out into the open, but, on the other, I felt like I'd betrayed my superiors and broken the chain of command by going behind their backs, speaking so openly to Bill Clementson. I suddenly found myself in a very lonely place, shouldering a burden I didn't feel I could share.

In the event, my meeting with Bill must have had the desired effect, as, by three o'clock that afternoon, word had come through that there *would*, after all, be a debrief, to be held at police HQ at 2pm the following Tuesday.

I later learned that it wasn't only pressure from Bill Clementson that had led to the climbdown; Ned Lawson had also lobbied the Executive for a debrief, outlining his concerns regarding the command-and-control element of the operation. He'd pointed out that the Firearms Manual stated quite clearly that, when involved in planning a firearms operation, the supervisory officer must consult a firearms tactical adviser. This, of course, hadn't happened during the Butsfield incident, and Ned concluded that, regrettably, the matter had to be brought out into the open. Although his was a considerably senior position, Ned's outspoken views nevertheless caused him to be isolated.

The following Tuesday, the conference room at HQ filled up as just about everybody who had been involved in the Butsfield incident filed in. Bill Lippett was there, together with John Taylor and Bob Gadd. This, I thought, was to be the moment of truth – not a trial or a witch hunt but an opportunity to learn from our mistakes. By two o'clock, there were about twenty-five people there, from the dog handler to the communications manager whose equipment had failed to meet the challenge required of it on the day.

A few minutes after two, Chief Superintendent Alan Miller entered the room with Superintendent Stan Hegarty by his side. (Was that it? Were they the only ones in senior management who were going to turn up?) Alan carefully explained that Assistant Chief Constable Eddie Marchant, who would normally have assumed the role of chairman, was on holiday but had left instructions for the format of the debrief.

From the outset, Alan Miller made it clear that the

debrief would cover only the elements of the incident itself and the subsequent events. There would be no discussion regarding the pre-planning of the operation. This statement created some consternation, principally amongst the firearms advisers, as well as many others there that afternoon.

Encouraged by his subordinates, Bill Lippett argued that they *should* talk about the planning and lack of advice, but Alan Miller responded curtly by repeating that there would be no talk about what had happened prior to the shooting at Butsfield, that it would be a matter for the council to mount such an inquiry.

That rather took the steam out of the whole proceedings. The organisation had, it seemed, decided to respond to the questions on everyone's lips with a deafening silence, and there wasn't a great deal left to talk about. Stan Hegarty said nothing and Ned Lawson sat to one side, looking about ready to explode.

So we were left with just the history of what had happened, as handed down from on high. There was a smattering of suggestions for a few minor procedural improvements, but the meeting was drawn to a close with almost indecent haste and, as we left the conference room, many of us felt that the constabulary had missed an opportunity to come to terms with an error of judgement that might well have prevented Harry Collinson's death. Needless to say, behind the closed door of the Support Services Department, there was some pretty vocal disapproval.

At Derwentside District Council, meanwhile, life had begun to return to normal, although the council workers couldn't escape the spotlight of publicity. Still numb, many found it difficult to come to terms with what had happened to their colleague and friend.

NALGO representative Joe Williamson was in close contact with the chief executive and personnel officer, and all three looked out for the employees' welfare however they could. It was very much a seat-of-the-pants situation, as none involved had ever been trained for such a situation and, to be fair, none of them had envisaged ever being in the position of having to look after staff who had been traumatised in such a manner. Joe concentrated on the three members of the planning department who had been directly involved in the events at Butsfield and quickly arranged for them and anyone else who needed it to receive counselling. (There was, in fact, little take-up for the offer, a reluctance that Joe put down to North-East macho culture.) The youngest of the three, Michael Allun, who had been filming the events of that day, had been severely affected, and he drifted around the council offices like a ghost, seemingly in a daze and answering only in monosyllables.

By now, the interests of the council and those of the union were beginning to diverge and NALGO called in its solicitors to protect its members, as people started to talk about civil proceedings against the council. As it later turned out, however, no claim was ever made, not even for criminal compensation.

By this time, the council had received many letters and telephone calls expressing condolence from across the country and even from abroad. Conversely, they had also received a large amount of hate mail blaming them for the arrest of Albert Dryden, described in one such letter as 'the little man who had stood up for his rights'. Comments had been openly made in and around Consett about the way in which the council had handled the incident, and it became apparent that there was a growing body of support for Albert Dryden. This groundswell of opinion in Consett was to gather considerable momentum in the coming weeks and months.

Meanwhile, Roy Collinson was asked to visit Neil Johnson, the council's chief executive, to discuss arrangements for Harry's funeral. Johnson had stated that the council would pay all of the funeral expenses, but Roy refused, knowing that his mother's wishes were that the occasion was to be, first and foremost, a family affair. Johnson argued that Harry was a well-liked and respected officer, and that the nationwide planning community wished to express its grief, and so Roy agreed that it would be appropriate to include the council in some capacity.

However, Roy then felt uncomfortable when Neil and Mike Bonser started to plan the funeral in front of him. The two council officials assumed that all of the members and employees would wish to pay their respects and agreed to shut down the council functions for the day of the funeral, at least until three o'clock. Obviously, given the number of people who might attend, the logistics of the funeral – which had been arranged to take place at 11am at Mounsett Crematorium, near Dipton, on Friday, 28 June 1991 – would be enormous. Mike and Neil then went on to start planning the parking arrangements in detail.

At this point, seeing the two council officials organise the bus and car parking required for his brother's funeral, Roy snapped. If that was what they wanted, then fine. Let them get on with it. He had his family to worry about.

In the event, the funeral went off without a hitch and Harry Collinson's body was finally laid to rest. It was, predictably, a momentous affair. So it was that Harry Collinson was finally laid to rest.

After the funeral, when Roy was sorting through Harry's possessions, he came across a poignant reminder of his brother: Harry's chequebook. Idly flicking through the stubs, he was once again struck by Harry's selflessness, even up to his death. One of his final acts had been to write out a cheque for £100, made out to Oxfam. That last cheque had left him £60 overdrawn.

FIFTEEN

Once arrested and charged with a serious offence, it is usual for the accused to be placed before a magistrates' court where he or she will be remanded to prison, to appear again, repeatedly, before that court until a trial date is fixed. This procedure usually takes a considerable amount of time, and in Dryden's case it was eight months before he finally met the jury. Twice he was taken to Derwentside Magistrates' Court to hear the charges against him read. As was usual with such serious cases, no application for bail was made. Meanwhile, he spent his days in Durham Prison, one of the more antique establishments within the British penal system.

Meanwhile, another dimension to the story was beginning to take shape. On the morning of the incident at Butsfield, local farmer's wife Jill Hall had intended to go to Dryden's farm and support him in his fight against the council but had been turned back at Eliza Lane by the police. After the shooting, still seeking to stand up for him, she decided to set up a petition to support the view that he'd been provoked beyond reason and that he'd been put in a position from which he couldn't back down, which had caused him to lose reason momentarily. She knew that he'd been charged and would be tried for murder; it was her goal to get the charge reduced to manslaughter. To this end, she produced posters and car-window stickers supporting her cause and circulated a petition, even buttonholing pedestrians in Consett town centre for signatures. It was claimed that, ultimately, over 3,000 signatures had been obtained.

I was taking my kids to school in Wolsingham one morning when I saw a car pass with a 'SUPPORT ALBERT DRYDEN' sticker displayed prominently in the back window. Incensed, I rushed over to the young mother driving the vehicle and harangued her about her insensitivity, pointing out that Harry Collinson's mother lived only fifty yards away. Horrified, she tore the sticker from the window.

The loose organisation of Dryden's supporters claimed that the whole of Consett was united in support of their beleaguered comrade. At one time, Jill Hall admitted that, while she was making all these efforts on Dryden's behalf, she was always conscious that her actions might hurt Collinson's family, but this didn't deter her from carrying on as, sorry though she was for them, she felt her cause was just.

Dryden's immediate family distanced themselves from Hall's support group, seeing their actions as serving only to fan the flames of the slumbering fire of Dryden's approaching trial. Elsie Donnelly, Dryden's sister, still felt comfortable moving around the town because everyone appeared so sympathetic, but she kept hearing one sentence on everyone's lips: 'This should never have happened.' She understood, however, that the Collinsons' grief would be equal to or greater than hers or that of her family and wisely kept her own counsel.

On the other side of the divide, the Collinsons were a very private family, as Harry had been, and their grief was similarly a very private matter. The family members rallied together and supported each other in the difficult time immediately after Harry's death. That's not to say, however, that the support for Dryden didn't reach the Collinson family and have a profound effect.

By the time of the second remand hearing, the support group, organised by Jill Hall, had gained momentum. On 3 July 1991, Dryden was led into the magistrates' court to roars of encouragement. At first, he looked bewildered by this, but he soon rose to the occasion and, full of bravado, responded with a two-fingered victory sign.

The court that day was crowded, the numbers swollen by around fifty of Dryden's supporters. The proceedings were limited to just a few short exchanges, each lasting no more than forty-five seconds, and the onlookers sat in silence throughout, as did Dryden himself, while outside his supporters tried to collect more signatures, loudly protesting the part played in the incident by Derwentside District Council.

Later that day, after the remand hearing, John Graham, who had been standing next to Harry when he had been shot, and Alf Lister, another friend of Dryden's, led a crowd to Derwentside Civic Centre (while escorted by a senior police officer), where they asked to see the council's chief executive, Neil Johnson. When he came down to see them, the two men thrust a letter into his hand. Neil thanked them tersely and vanished inside without further comment. He went back to his office, where he read the letter carefully and then showed it to Mike Bonser.

The letter was a request for the council to hold a formal inquiry – 'sooner rather than later' – into the events leading up to the shooting.

Meanwhile, Dryden himself wasn't short of visitors. Jill Hall visited him on a number of occasions while he was on remand in Durham Prison, as did his old friend George Cameron frequently. After one such visit, George told a newspaper reporter, 'I saw Albert in prison. He was bearing up, but when you put someone who is used to being outdoors in a cell 8ft by 8ft, it has an effect. We talked for a while, but he broke down at the end. He doesn't know what to make of all the support. He didn't know he had so many friends.'

Dryden's mood fluctuated considerably while he was in prison, his demeanour veering from being reasonably cheerful to suicidal. Indeed, at times he was placed on suicide watch, checked on every fifteen minutes by a prison officer. He also complained endlessly about his confinement as a category A prisoner, with its accompanying restrictive regime, moaning, 'I get nothing to do. I sit in the cell all day. I hope to have a heart attack or a brain haemorrhage. All my interest in life has gone. I'm just like a tree stump, sitting in there.'

Dryden also alleged that he'd succumbed to pneumonia and pleurisy twice during his confinement, and claimed that he had nightmares and heard voices. He still couldn't hold himself responsible for the killing, though, and protested that he hadn't been aware that he had done it, later extending this claim to attest that some evil force had taken over his body. How much this was a calculated ploy to add weight to any defence argument is debatable.

As the support group continued to paint a damning picture of the council as the aggressor and of Harry Collinson as its malevolent agent, their attempts to turn Dryden into a Bonnie-and-Clyde-style anti-hero were condemned by NALGO. Joe Williamson stated in the press that, after such a tragedy, such an attack on the bureaucracy and the personnel involved was more than distasteful, adding, 'The use of this tragedy to mount an attack on the officers of local authorities is an affront to all NALGO members.' It was rare for such a normally staid group to become so riled.

Eventually, on Monday, 16 March 1992, the trial of the case of *Regina versus Albert Dryden* began at the Crown

Court, in the Moot Hall, Newcastle-upon-Tyne, with the Honourable Mrs Justice Ebsworth presiding. It was made clear there that Dryden had been charged by Chief Inspector Arthur Proud with the murder of Harry Collinson and the attempted murder of Michael Dunstan, Tony Belmont and PC Steven Campbell.

Court hearings are conducted upon an imposing stage and are full of ritual and tradition that, to the uninformed eye, can appear very intimidating. On this occasion, centre-stage, were two men who, bewigged and gowned, would dissect the evidence and their witnesses' testimonies, looking for the slightest chink in the armour of their opponent's case. Appearing for the prosecution was Mr John Milford, QC (who has since gone on to become a judge), while representing Dryden was Mr James Chadwin, QC, who attained some notoriety by defending the Yorkshire Ripper, Peter Sutcliffe. Both were extremely experienced counsel, eminently qualified for their roles in the courtroom drama that was about to unfold.

There were to be thirty-one witnesses called on behalf of the prosecution and six for the defence, including Dryden himself.

A number of Dryden's supporters crowded the public gallery, and he waved at them as he mounted the steps into the dock from the cells below, asking them if they didn't think he looked smart. He'd been out the previous night, he told them, to a local gents' outfitters to buy a new jacket and slacks for the occasion. (The fact that his jocular manner didn't reflect the seriousness of his situation was later remarked on. It was suggested that he felt himself detached from the proceedings, the implication being that he wasn't wholly aware of what was going on.)

Then the judge came into the courtroom and a hush fell. Dryden stood in the dock, a slight, bearded figure with hollow, staring eyes, pale from lack of sunlight. As the charges against him were read out and his pleas were requested, he replied almost belligerently, 'Not guilty, your honour,' to each allegation laid against him. Then a prison officer laid his hand on Dryden's shoulder and gently eased him back into his seat.

John Milford, the prosecuting lawyer, then got to his feet, shuffled his papers, adjusted his wig and began to summarise the evidence that would be presented to the court. He warned the six men and six women of the jury to push any recollections of the media coverage of the killing out of their minds and consider the evidence afresh. He then described Dryden's long-running planning dispute with Derwentside District Council, making a pointed reference to *Evening Chronicle* reporter Garry Willey's warning to the police that Dryden might resort to violence on the day of the demolition.

Then the most compelling piece of evidence was presented: the video footage shot by the BBC *Look North* news crew in which Dryden had pointedly warned Harry Collinson, 'You might not be around to see the outcome of this disaster.' Milford chillingly told the jury how Collinson was shot deliberately, and in precise detail he described Dryden climbing through the fence, gun in hand, and how he had recklessly fired his pistol indiscriminately at the fleeing crowd, wounding Belmont and Campbell in the process. Finally, he gave a heart-stopping account of how Dryden had returned to Collinson's inert body and, calmly and deliberately, fired two further shots into the council worker's corpse.

By now, the court was hanging on his every word, and in a matter-of-fact tone Milford went on to recount the sequence of events that had brought Dryden before the court – of how Dryden had been arrested, taken to Consett Police Station and then later interviewed by DCI Proud. He then gave the jury a piercing look and observed, 'A more deliberate murder would be hard to imagine.'

The video footage was then played again in slow motion and freeze frame as the counsel demonstrated all the witnesses' positions at the moment when Collinson had been killed, and Milford pointed out to the twelve jury members before him, 'You may think that there is little dispute about his intention, since he shot him not once, or twice, but three times.'

Next, Milford spoke about the underscanning technique that the police had used, which had revealed that it had been Dryden's intention to murder Michael Dunstan, the council's solicitor, too. The jury watched the video coverage one more time, looking on impassively.

Towards the end of that day's session, the court heard from Michael Dunstan himself. A legal professional normally accustomed to a court environment, he was unused to playing the role of a witness and was described by onlookers that day as appearing distressed, red in the face and sweating profusely as he gave his evidence. The reliving of the horror of Butsfield was evidently taking its toll. Dunstan confirmed that he had advised the council's officers that, if there was violence, or any threat of violence, they should retreat from any confrontation and he would then seek a High Court injunction. He also attested that, during his dealings with Dryden, he recalled that there had been no apparent animosity, and that the events at Butsfield were, to his mind, completely unprecedented. Dryden had even called him Michael on the morning of the shooting.

At this point, the judge decided to conclude the first day's proceedings and warned the jury sternly not to discuss the case. All the participants dispersed and Dryden was taken down the steps to return to prison.

Many of the witnesses had been required to attend the trial right from the beginning, including the three council officers. They had gathered that first day at Joe Williamson's office (as they would continue to do until their evidence had been heard), then walked the short distance to the Moot Hall, being forced to pass through a crowd of Dryden's family and supporters outside the court. While there was no direct hostility towards any of the witnesses attending the trial by the crowds outside the court, there was a tangible air of sullen resentment.

At the request of his superiors in the union, Williamson attended the whole trial, taking notes, for which he had to ask the judge's permission – an intimidating task, as he had to stand and identify himself first, then explain the reasons behind his request. At the end of each day, he would hand his notes to the court usher, who would return them to him the following morning.

At the beginning of the trial's second day, Michael Dunstan again took the stand and began by re-emphasising the council's position in the enforcement proceedings. 'I was satisfied that they were legally entitled to do this,' he later explained. 'I had no doubts about it.'

In later cross-examination, defence lawyer James Chadwin asked Dunstan whether he recalled a meeting between the council and the police two days before the killing, during which the police had allegedly been unenthusiastic about the notion of proceeding with the demolition. Dunstan stated he didn't recall any such opinion being given, although the police *had* been in favour of not telling Dryden the date and time of the demolition.

John Milford then moved on to the wounding of the two other men. BBC journalist Tony Belmont told the court that, as he'd turned to flee for his life, a bullet had hit his right arm, splintering bone and sending a huge surge of pain up his shoulder. He told how he'd undergone emergency surgery, during which his nerve endings had been repaired and a fragment of bone had been removed from his arm, before going on to inform the jury that he'd needed a further four operations on his shattered limb. 'There was a mêlée and a panic,' he recalled. 'People were running for their lives. I just had a feeling that I had to leave; I had to get out of there because the pain was quite tremendous. I was afraid I might collapse and be shot again. As I was running, the pain seemed to subside. There is a fear and a panic that sets in when you're running for your life, literally, and then the pain came back again.'

After Belmont stood down, Steven Campbell – the second person to have been wounded at Butsfield – stepped up to the stand, the first police officer to do so at the trial thus far. He stood up ramrod straight in his uniform and looked directly at the judge, then identified Dryden in a voice filled with emotion and simply told his story: 'I was running as fast as I could, considering I had a full uniform on. I got shot in the lower back, but I tried to keep on running.'

The court then heard from Mr Jocelyn, the foreman of the contractors W&M Thompson of Prudhoe, who had been brought in to carry out the demolition. Jocelyn stated that he and a colleague had watched as Dryden and Collinson argued by the gate. When negotiations broke down, he remembered thinking that the operation should be abandoned and his workmate telling him, 'This is the time to go.' Instead, Collinson had instructed them both to unload the excavator and have it ready to break through the fence around Dryden's land. 'Then,' Jocelyn remembered, 'all hell was let loose.'

John Milford then called his next witness, Helen Dodd, an administration officer at Consett County Court who'd met Dryden when he'd been contemplating a court action against Harry Collinson for trespassing and taking photographs unauthorised. Dodd testified that, after she'd advised Dryden to consult a solicitor, he'd left her office, saying, 'I'll take a gun to the lot of them.' She hadn't taken him seriously.

Next, planning technician Michael Allun, one of Joe Williamson's charges, took the stand. He told the jury that he'd been there only to take photographs of what was happening in case the dispute between the council and Dryden ever went to court, and how he'd been just yards away when Dryden had fired his gun at Collinson. At one stage, he admitted, when Dryden had looked in his direction, still holding the loaded weapon, he'd feared for his own life.

Allun then told the jury that he'd seen Collinson's body after it had been shot the second time. 'I couldn't tell if he was dead or not... He looked in a pretty bad way. There might have been slight twitches.'

After Allun had left the stand, he was replaced by his colleague, Grant Atkinson, who told the court that Harry had been lying in the ditch, eyes open, hands clutching two clumps of grass, and that he'd seen blood on Harry's shirt and chest. 'I held his wrist briefly but, looking in his face, there seemed to be no sign of life.'

Finally, John Shepherd of the Council Engineers' Department took the stand to conclude this grim catalogue of recollection.

Day three of the trial began with the testimony of *Evening Chronicle* reporter Garry Willey's chilling prophecy of the

events at Butsfield that he gave to the police after visiting
Dryden at his home in Priestman Avenue. He'd originally
gone to see Dryden, he said, in order to get a reaction
from him to the news that the date had been set for his
bungalow to be demolished, and he admitted that he knew
Dryden was usually good for a sensational quote. 'Towards
the end of this list of various reasons why the bungalow
would still be there, he said he had the wherewithal to
protect the bungalow with force,' Willey reported. 'He left
the doorstep and returned inside the house somewhere
and came back holding what looked to me like a spent
bullet, about three inches long, made of brass. He
described it as a "full metal jacket". He said he had a
machine gun and had been out on the moors at Stanhope,
practising, and the weapon was powerful enough to cut
through the JCB and the driver with it. He said that, if
Harry Collinson went through with the demolition or
tried to come on his land, he would burn him and he
would burn his wife at the stake.'

This was one of only a few moments during the trial
when Dryden became agitated.

Willey then went on to recall other colourful interviews
that he'd conducted with Dryden, including one in which
Dryden had told Willey of his intent to blow up the Civic
Centre. 'They would be running out of body bags,' Willey
quoted him.

By now scenting blood, John Milford called George
Cameron, described as Dryden's oldest and closest friend,
who timidly took the stand and then proceeded to give his

evidence, prompted by the prosecution, through a veil of tears. He'd been beside Dryden as the heated exchange had escalated, he admitted. Whether through shock or fear, he'd done nothing to stop his friend's rampage, he confessed, but had stayed close to him throughout. As Dryden had reloaded his revolver, he'd pressed six spent cartridge cases in Cameron's hand and said to him, 'There's some souvenirs.' On that day, when he had seen his friend with the pistol, which he recognised so well, Cameron had thought at first that Dryden was about to take his own life in a blaze of publicity, pleading that he'd had no idea that he might shoot anyone else.

In his later cross-examination of Cameron, setting the stage for the defence argument, James Chadwin led him into speculation as to whether the Albert Dryden he'd known all his life was the same Albert Dryden who had killed Harry Collinson that day. 'No,' sobbed Cameron.

The prosecution then called to the witness stand another supporter and friend of Dryden, Henry Thomas, who had first met the defendant only the previous January. Thomas gave evidence that supported the charge of attempted murder, reporting that, on the day of the incident, having shot Collinson, Dryden had seemed to retreat into a world of his own and that he'd heard him repeating over and over, 'like a gramophone', that he was going to get Michael Dunstan. Thomas testified that he'd followed Dryden down the road, trying to persuade him to part with the gun. Far from helping Dryden with his testimony, however, Thomas merely confirmed the defendant's intent to murder the council's solicitor.

The police evidence was then called. First, the hapless police commander that day, Superintendent Stan Hegarty, was called to the stand. He proceeded to tell the court that, at the meeting two days before the shooting, he'd explained to council officials the limitations on police powers in such circumstances and how, despite the enforcement notice served on Dryden, they'd be powerless to remove him, even if he went as far as to sit in front of the bulldozer, because he owned the land and they had no legal right to touch him. Hegarty confirmed that he'd clearly outlined that the police's position was strictly an impartial one in what had been essentially a civil matter between the council and Dryden. However, he observed, if the dispute eventually came before the High Court and an injunction had been obtained, with an accompanying power of arrest, it would have been a different matter. 'We were merely to be there to prevent a breach of the peace occurring,' Hegarty attested. 'It was clear to me at the end of the meeting that we'd come to the agreement that, if any resistance was offered, peaceful or otherwise, the council would withdraw and seek an injunction.'

Then, under cross-examination by the defence lawyer, Hegarty surprisingly admitted that he'd been very concerned about a possible confrontation between Dryden and the council. Of course, if that was indeed the case, the unasked question was, exactly what level of violence had he anticipated that day, considering that he'd decided to have armed officers available?

Hegarty hadn't been at Butsfield on the day of the shooting; he'd been back at Consett Police Station, in contact with Inspector Geoff Young, who'd been controlling events on the ground. On hearing a garbled message that had mentioned firearms, however, he'd rushed to Eliza Lane, where Hegarty testified that he'd heard gunshots. At this point, he'd taken cover with Young and waited for the ARV to arrive.

The rest of the day was taken up with the brief testimonies of PCs Andy Reay and Phil Brown, the armed-response officers, and of Sergeant John Taylor, the arresting officer. Before the close of business, an expert witness, forensic scientist Malcolm Fletcher, took the stand and identified the murder weapon, pouring cold water on Dryden's self-claimed abilities as a gunsmith by describing him as merely 'someone who tinkers with weapons' and dismissing the defendant's boast that he never missed a man's head from ninety yards as 'a pretty strong claim'.

The next day, it was Arthur Proud's turn to take the stand. He presented himself well in the witness box as an intelligent, experienced officer and told the jury in calm, measured tones how he'd first met Dryden many years earlier and had come to like him, regarding him at that time as a colourful local character. He told them of Dryden's unfounded allegations of council corruption and his attitude of suspicion and bitterness towards authority.

He then told them how he admired Dryden's ability to recall dates and minutiae, describing him as possibly one of the most organised and collected men he'd ever met. But that had been at a different time and place, and that had been a different Albert Dryden.

Arthur recounted the details of the interviews that had taken place after Dryden's arrest, in which Dryden had described Collinson as an evil and nasty man who hadn't been prepared to listen to reason. Then the jury heard a tape-recording of the second interview, in which Arthur was heard to say, 'You have been calm, collected and rational. You have behaved in a way that I am surprised about, Albert. I would have expected a bit of remorse out of you.' The tape hissed as Arthur's comment met with only silence from the accused.

The jury listened further to the verbal duel between Proud and Dryden, in which Dryden's responses became more cautious and considered when faced with pointed questions.

Then the recording of the third interview was played and the jury heard the breakthrough that Proud had been waiting for when Dryden was heard to say, 'I believe I did do it, but I don't know why I done it.'

The recording of Arthur's disembodied voice revealed only the slightest tremor as he asked Dryden, '*Have* you shot him?'

'I probably have,' Dryden answered.

After that, the rest of Arthur Proud's evidence was somewhat academic. The defence lawyer asked a few perfunctory questions and it was reported that Dryden had heard voices in his cell and saw an apparition of Harry Collinson sitting there, although it was also noted that Dryden had never mentioned that he'd suffered from any other hallucinations prior to that day.

So concluded the first week of the trial and, with it, the prosecution's evidence in chief. The stage was set for Dryden's appearance in the witness box the following week.

SIXTEEN

On Monday morning, the courtroom at Newcastle Crown Court was packed as Dryden took the stand, looking shabby and slightly pathetic. Taking the Bible in his hand, he looked defiantly around the room, his self-importance visibly swelling within him as he spoke the oath.

It was then the unenviable task of the defence counsel, James Chadwin – only too aware of the volatile nature of his main witness – to lead Dryden delicately through his evidence.

Dryden began by describing how he'd first got to know Harry during friendly chats over cups of tea. 'I thought he was a gentleman,' he told the jury. 'He gave us all the attention I wanted. He seemed first class, like.'

Then he told the jury that Collinson had regularly

visited his smallholding at Eliza Lane, giving Dryden tips on tree planting. It was during one of these visits, said Dryden, that Collinson had advised him that he didn't need planning permission to construct a greenhouse, a potting shed or a building for livestock.

Dryden then mentioned that he'd made regular visits to Collinson in his office, where he had always been warmly welcomed with a cup of tea and a biscuit, and that he and Collinson had become very friendly. He recalled that he'd once invited Collinson over for a drink and had even offered to let him drive one of his Cadillacs, although he couldn't remember whether Collinson had taken him up on either offer.

Dryden claimed that things had begun to turn sour between them when Collinson had 'led him up the garden path' in the planning wrangle that had developed and that, having allegedly given him verbal permission for his building, Collinson then turned against him because he feared for his job. He had first mentioned the bungalow idea in 1987, apparently, but had then been told that planning permission would be refused on the grounds that his land was too small to enable him to make a living from agriculture. Undeterred, however, Dryden planned his underground house after seeing a television feature about a man who had succeeded with such a venture and hadn't needed planning permission.

Dryden told the court of how he had informed Collinson of his intention before starting work on the bungalow, and the planner had allegedly said that there wouldn't be any problem with him building such a structure, but he didn't seem convinced that Dryden would actually go through with it.

According to Dryden, council officials had visited him while he was working on the site but didn't suggest that he was doing anything wrong until April 1989, when he received a letter from Collinson's superior telling him to take all of his buildings down. Upset, Dryden went in to see Collinson about the letter. 'Collinson said, "I've denied knowing anything about it,"' Dryden quoted to the court. '"I can't pull any more strings. My job's in jeopardy."'

From that point on, said Dryden, the relationship between him and Collinson degenerated further after the latter failed to appear at a planning inquiry in January 1990. Dryden told of bitter arguments that followed in which foul language was used by both parties. He even started civil proceedings against Collinson for trespass, harassment and illegal photography on his land.

Dryden also told the jury that he'd suffered an acute pain in his head and that he'd feared a brain haemorrhage on the day that Collinson had died, although he did accept that he fired the fatal shots. 'Well, I think it's a tragedy,' he replied when asked how he felt about that. 'It could have been avoided. It should never have happened. It was because they decided to take the law into their own hands and not back off. They just wouldn't wait a few more weeks, and it all turned out very badly.' This was the closest Dryden would come to remorse for Collinson's death throughout the trial.

Dryden then went on to deny that he had told *Evening Chronicle* reporter Garry Willey in the days before the shooting that he would burn Mr Collinson and then burn his wife at the stake. 'Definitely not!' he protested, almost shouting. 'He is a liar. He is a stranger to the truth!'

James Chadwin then asked Dryden if he felt that Collinson had deserved to die, and the defendant thought for a moment before replying, 'Nobody deserves to get killed. Everybody has to die, but nobody deserves to be killed.'

On the shooting of Tony Belmont, he admitted, 'I'm very sorry it happened – very, very sorry. If it hadn't been for Mr Collinson telling people about the event, they would never have been there.' And when asked about wounding PC Steven Campbell, Dryden said again that he was very sorry, adding, 'If I'd been in a right frame of mind and I'd been all right, that wouldn't have happened.' This was to be Dryden's sole apology throughout the trial.

When asked what he'd thought when he'd seen all the media present on the day of the shooting, Dryden said, 'I felt as though they were going to humiliate us in front of millions of people. It looked as though they were going to make a film. They didn't realise what they were doing. And I think Mr Collinson was going to make an example of us.'

John Milford then began his cross-examination, suggesting at first that Dryden had exaggerated Harry Collinson's behaviour by implying that he'd used foul and abusive language to him. However, Dryden maintained that, during an incident on his land in March 1991, Collinson had behaved like 'a beast'. Then, when Milford asked Dryden if he was comfortable referring to a man whom he had killed in such a way, and asked him if he'd ever thought about the fact that Mr Collinson had been a father of two, Dryden admitted that, on Christmas Day that year, he'd sat in his hospital-wing cell and thought about how Collinson might have spent Christmas with his family. He was not, he asserted, a man of violence.

By this time, Dryden's attitude had become even more agitated and he was giving vent to occasional bursts of anger, and Milford seized every opportunity to demonstrate Dryden's irascible nature. After a number of outbursts of colourful language, Dryden apologised for using such language to the judge, who acknowledged his apology but advised him to curb his tongue.

Arthur Proud had testified that, while on remand, Dryden had confessed to hearing voices and having suicidal thoughts, and Milford pressed the defendant on this claim, asking him, 'Is it true, Mr Dryden, or is it an invention of aberrant behaviour to support the contention that it is really mental illness which lies behind the enormity of your behaviour?' Dryden, of course, denied such manipulative behaviour.

Soon Milford had finished questioning Dryden, and then the defendant's GP, Dr Donald Chapman, was called to the stand. Chapman proceeded to inform the jury that, nine days before the shooting, he'd examined Dryden, who'd looked to be 'near the end of his tether', complaining of sleeplessness and anxiety. He'd struck Dr Chapman as being very nervous, very agitated and almost frightened, so he'd prescribed a course of mild tranquillisers, although he admitted that he hadn't thought that anti-depressants were necessary, nor had he seen the need to make an appointment for his patient to see a consultant psychiatrist.

Over the next few days, much was made of Albert Dryden's state of mind at the time of the incident. People that knew him or had come into contact with him both before and after the event used many terms to describe him, from simply 'agitated' to 'cold-blooded' and 'evil'. In his attempt to reduce the charge of murder to one of manslaughter, Dryden's counsel produced extensive psychiatric evidence supposedly supporting his client's claim that he'd been acting under diminished responsibility at the time of the offence. To this end, James Chadwin had employed the services of three separate experts: Dr Peter Wood, a psychiatrist from Bradford; Dr Lesley Burton, then working from St Luke's Hospital in Middlesbrough; and Eric Wright, a chartered forensic psychologist, also from Bradford.

In response to this, the prosecution took steps to rebut this evidence with that of their own experts, Dr Hamish McClelland, a consultant psychiatrist working for Newcastle Health Trust, and Dr Paul Bowden, a consultant forensic psychiatrist working from Bethlem Royal Hospital and Maudsley Hospital in Denmark Hill, London.

All three defence psychiatrists/psychologists were called to give evidence, but only Dr McClelland appeared for the prosecution. Even so, to say that the psychiatric evaluation of Albert Dryden took some considerable time would be to understate things massively.

The first witness called for the defence was Dr Burton, a tall, striking, imperious figure who had been asked to examine Dryden after his arrest and prepare a thorough report on his medical history and his current physical condition. Interviewing Dryden, it appeared, had turned out to be a slow, tiring exercise. The first of their three interviews lasted about an hour and a half, during which Dr Burton had just let Dryden talk. Whenever the doctor tried to move him on or change direction, Dryden would take off at a tangent, leaving the interview in tatters, so in the long run it proved easier to allow him to take things at his own pace.

After examining Dryden, Dr Burton felt able to give some testimony on his behalf. He pointed out that there was little doubt that the stress of his dispute with the council was compounded by the death of his mother in April 1990, causing him to develop symptoms of anxiety and tension, insomnia, poor concentration, depression, loss of appetite and weight, loss of interest in his work and hobbies (ie his cars), and a general tendency to neglect both his health and his personal appearance. In Dr Burton's opinion, Dryden had suffered from a very severe reactive depression for some two years prior to the alleged offence. For three to four weeks prior to the incident, he could well have been in a borderline psychotic state. The combination of these two traumatic events could easily have caused an abnormality of mind, argued Dr Burton, which could have then substantially impaired Dryden's sense of responsibility. However, he did qualify this view by adding that Dryden hadn't apparently been suffering from any defect of reason or from any mental disorder at the time of the shooting.

It was clear that, with the assistance of the defence psychiatrists, the defence counsel was seeking to have the current charge of murder reduced to one of manslaughter on the grounds of diminished responsibility, which would incur either a suspended sentence or a probation order. This wasn't a realistic position, however, and would prove a mountainous obstacle for Dryden's defence team.

During the second week of the trial, Dr Burton felt obliged to inform Dryden that, if he were convicted on a charge of manslaughter on the grounds of diminished responsibility, the prosecution would then probably consult a specialist psychiatrist to determine the feasibility of a secure hospital order. Dryden didn't react happily to this news, to say the least, and there was a sudden dramatic deep shift in his enthusiasm towards psychiatrists.

After the trial, Dr Burton observed that Dryden had appeared to have had no subsequent recall of his actions covering a very brief period before he shot Collinson, and opined that it was unlikely that Dryden was using this as a convenient device, as it wasn't uncommon for people to be unable to recall events in similarly traumatic situations.

He then cited a well-documented incident involving a man named Gunter Doler, who in 1959 had shot a policeman and then claimed to have no memory of the event. Doler had been judged fit to stand trial, however, and his defence was set aside because subsequent memory loss couldn't be held to have affected his prior actions. This was equally true of Dryden's situation.

Dr Burton went on to state that he didn't believe Dryden had ever shown true remorse for Collinson's murder, although the defendant had admitted that he was sorry that the council worker had been killed without actually taking any personal responsibility for his death. Possibly, it hadn't been Dryden's intention to shoot Harry Collinson as an individual but as the physical representation of Derwentside District Council. However, the jury didn't appreciate this fine distinction.

Dr Burton noted that he'd found Dryden to be a very rigid man with peculiar yet clear-cut views. Throughout his life, Dryden had been unable to cope with authority in any form, the doctor observed, and would interpret matters according to his own internal set of rules, which often left him frustrated and angry, as demonstrated within the courtroom. 'On day one of his trial,' said Dr Burton, 'it was quite clear that Albert was talking about the fact that, if he got manslaughter and got a probation order, he might be able to visit his sister in Canada later that year. I don't think he fully appreciated what was going on. I don't think he came across as a very good witness in the box. I think he rather lost his rag, and I suspect that that didn't go down well with the jury. Certainly, this was an element to him that I hadn't seen. When he was in the witness box, there was a degree of hostility that wasn't there during interviews, and I don't think he did himself any favours.'

It was then psychiatrist Dr Peter Wood's turn to give his diagnosis of Dryden's mental state. He reported that, when he'd interviewed Dryden, the patient's attitude towards the council had been one of paranoid belligerence. Dryden had suspected that unidentified people had been keeping a special watch on his land for various reasons, saying that they had 'switched their cars and used binoculars and the like in order to keep a very close eye on him'.

Dr Wood then reported that Dryden had also stated that, on eleven occasions over the weekend prior to the scheduled demolition, he had played a solitary game of Russian roulette, taking his survival as being something akin to divine intervention and an indication that he should carry on the fight – a common attitude displayed by active depressives, said the doctor.

Dr Wood also noted that he rarely encountered people who were quite as eccentric as Dryden. Every examined aspect of the defendant's life revealed marked eccentricities, whether in his relationships with others, his hobbies, his way of life or his general appearance. His attitude, judged Dr Wood, could be described as 'bizarre', convincing him that Dryden had been suffering from major mental illness and that he was suffering from an abnormality of mind through a combination of disease and inherent causes, resulting in a severe impairment of his sense of responsibility for his own actions on the day of the shooting. At that point, suggested Dr Wood, stresses had overwhelmed Dryden's ability to think rationally, and inability to remember what had happened at the time arose from a genuine amnesia associated with his abnormal mental state.

(Before the trial had begun, Dr Wood had advised Dryden to plead guilty to a charge of manslaughter on the grounds of diminished responsibility – sound advice that Dryden had evidently ignored. That final contradiction went some way to salvaging what could have been a damaging piece of testimony to the prosecution.)

Dr Wood then went on to relate the details of further interviews he'd conducted with Dryden. On one occasion, the defendant appeared to have been quite cheerful, making grand statements concerning his plans for the future. He'd suggested selling his land to build a hotel on it, noted Dr Wood, possibly with the help of a European Community grant – clearly grossly unrealistic behaviour, judged the doctor. Dryden had then mentioned his plans to tarmac his drive and spoke at length about various prosecution witnesses being in league with each other, belonging to the same union and getting together in a 'special way' to get their stories straight. At times, observed Dr Wood, he seemed quite brittle, yet boastful and arrogant, exaggerating his own position as a self-perceived martyr. Dr Wood stated that, overall, he agreed with Dr Burton's diagnosis, although he judged Dryden's condition to be more extreme than his colleague believed.

The last defence witness to give evidence about Dryden's psychiatric assessment was forensic psychologist Eric Wright, who had carried out a number of tests to determine Dryden's intelligence quotient. The average IQ in the adult population is 100, while average intelligence is held as being between 90 and 109 and 50 per cent of the adult population would be expected to have IQ within that range. In his tests, Dryden achieved a score of 88 – below the average range. He was, however, extremely precise and quick to respond when asked general questions. When asked, for example, the distance from London to New York, he replied 2,680 miles (it's actually 3,471 miles); when asked what the population of the United Kingdom was, he replied 64 million (actually 56 million); and when asked the temperature at which water boils, he replied 280 degrees Fahrenheit (actually 212 degrees). The accuracy of Dryden's answers impressed Mr Wright less than the confident, precise and obsessive manner in which they were delivered.

What wasn't reported, however, was the fact that, during his interview with Mr Wright, Dryden had hinted that there was something bigger to come after the trial, that he could see himself becoming 'dictator of England'. He likened himself to Fidel Castro and stated that, if he could, he'd carry a sub-machine gun with him everywhere he went. He even suggested that the Prime Minister should be taught how to use one, too, and should carry one with him at all times.

After Mr Wright had stepped down, it was the

prosecution's turn to call their witnesses. First up was consultant psychiatrist Dr Hamish McClelland, who had established that Dryden was a happy individual, by and large, if something of a worrier, obsessing over little things. "'If a door needed a coat of paint,'" quoted McClelland, "'it would remain in my mind.'" In interview, Dryden said that he was very particular about the way things were done, claiming that he was a good timekeeper at work – a slow worker, but very careful in what he did – describing how he would assiduously plan each day as he rose in the morning. When questioned about his temper, he claimed that he'd never been known to lose it and that it was in his nature to back away rather than confront anyone.

It was clear from the documentation chronicling Dryden's conflict with Derwentside District Council that the defendant had become increasingly bitter, angry and paranoid, but it was Dr McClelland's opinion that this hadn't developed into a paranoid psychosis, and he could find no evidence that Dryden's thinking had become delusional. Dryden was a man who followed his own logic and principles, and his conviction that he was in the right had been fuelled by the support given by his relatives and friends.

Dr McClelland then went on to recall how Dryden had come across as being very relaxed during interview, prepared to talk happily about his past life and interests, displaying an attitude that fostered an easy, sympathetic relationship between psychiatrist and patient. He was pedantic in the extreme, of course, and picky about giving precise dates and measurements and every conceivable detail about his history. "'I have a terrific memory,'" Dr McClelland quoted, "'like Lesley Welch on the radio – the Memory Man. I'm as good as him. But I think my mind is too quick.'"

Indeed, Dryden's quickness of mind, combined with his tendency to talk at length without pause, led to some problems in his interviews with Dr McClelland (just as they had in his discussions with Dr Burton), where Dryden demonstrated his fondness of repetition and extravagant gestures and at times was almost impossible to interrupt. He had something of an 'ancient mariner' quality about him, Dr McClelland judged, and his intense manner of speech was associated with anger, a man convinced of his own rectitude.

Dr McClelland stated that Dryden had come across as being self-satisfied and arrogant. His life hadn't been one of material success, the doctor noted, and so he sought validation for his skills in rocketry and as a gunsmith, marksman and builder – all disciplines in which he hailed himself as an expert in an attempt, said the doctor, to compensate him for his failures in ordinary life.

During his interviews with Dr McClelland, it had become clear that Dryden was a man of limited intelligence who would talk in terms of 'concrete thinking without any lateral meaning, only dealing in specifics, and his range of general vocabulary was limited'. Dr McClelland then conducted a second IQ test, similar to the first set by Mr Wright, in which Dryden managed to achieve only the meagre score of 77.

Dr McClelland then testified that, in his considered opinion, he could detect no evidence that Dryden was suffering from a serious mental illness. Certainly, the defendant was unhappy and must have been depressed, but not so far as to cause retardation or agitation, and his depression hadn't progressed into delusional thinking. Dryden continued to assert that he had 'snapped' at the time of the tragedy, and that he was pushed into it, but was adamant that he'd felt no aggression towards Collinson. According to his twisted logic, he'd been pushed beyond his limits, and so the killing wasn't his fault.

Tellingly, Dryden showed no remorse for the killing and accepted no guilt whatsoever. Indeed, in his mind he'd disassociated himself from it altogether, lamenting, 'It could have been avoided. It should never have happened.' Throughout the trial, Dryden would abrogate all responsibility for events, including his own shooting rampage, responsibility for which he would attempt to pass off on to all the other agencies and people involved.

In his dealings with Dryden, Dr McClelland had found him to be a very self-righteous man, never once expressing doubts about his opinions or behaviour. In the doctor's opinion, the defendant saw himself as being at the centre of a vast, dramatic scenario in which he was forced to defend his homestead. Also, at the time of the shooting there had been friends and relatives present, so it could be possible that Dryden didn't want to lose face in front of

DEATH ON A SUMMER'S DAY

them. There were also reporters and cameramen present, as well as people he detested, a fact that may well have made it difficult for him to back down. It was only this factor, judged Dr McClelland, that caused his hatred of Collinson – both for his personal actions and because he represented the council – to tip him over into displaying homicidal tendencies. He couldn't cope with the situation. But, argued the doctor, he didn't go berserk; instead, he descended into a controlled and determined phase of behaviour, going about the shooting in a purposeful way. The only period in which it could be argued that he was out of control, said McClelland, was when he shot wildly in Eliza Lane. Following this, he regained his composure and returned to Collinson's body, into which he fired two further shots.

Dryden's claim of amnesia, that he couldn't remember anything about the incident, was unlikely to be true, said Dr McClelland, as according to all the witness statements taken after the incident he'd been completely aware of what he'd been doing at the time. Of course, qualified the doctor, he might now wish to suppress the incident from his conscious mind.

Dr McClelland concluded that, having considered all the evidence, he didn't consider that Dryden had been suffering from any depressive illness, even when this diagnosis took into account his decidedly eccentric personality and limited intelligence, and so a defence of substantially diminished responsibility couldn't be justified, in his opinion.

Seeing a possible glimmer of light, James Chadwin leaped on Dr McClelland's diagnosis. 'If we took out the word "substantially",' he suggested, 'was Mr Dryden's responsibility for that killing diminished?' This was obviously an exercise in semantics, and Dr McClelland was forced to agree but forcibly qualified his answer by saying that the concept on which he'd been asked to give expert witness was that of 'substantially' diminished responsibility, and as such he would stand by his opinion.

The Crown Prosecution Service had stipulated that Dryden should also be examined by a consultant forensic psychiatrist, in this case a Mr Paul Bowden, who wasn't in fact called as a witness, although his statement was disclosed to the defence counsel. It turned out that the life history Mr Bowden took of Dryden and the psychiatrist's initial observations very much reflected those of Dr McClelland. Notably, however, when Mr Bowden asked him to describe his own personality, Dryden had replied that he was an 'individualist', that he disapproved of religious organisations and that, given the opportunity, he would bulldoze churches and cathedrals and get rid of what he saw as the parasitic clergy. He also felt that political parties should be abolished and replaced by military dictators, like Castro, and that armed aggression should be used to displace governments, expressing some admiration for Adolf Hitler. Mr Bowden's notes reveal that Dryden had enthused about weapons and other militaria and expressed his belief that he'd been born at the wrong time; fifty years earlier and he would have been acknowledged as an expert on ballistics and automatic weapons and treated with the respect that was his due.

Dryden also claimed to Mr Bowden that he had no memory of the shootings and wouldn't accept any evidence supporting the indication that his actions might have been premeditated. The psychiatrist described him as having an unusual personality, characterised by eccentricity, intolerance, single-mindedness, inventiveness and obsessiveness, while further tests had his IQ pegged at just 80.

At this point, Mr Bowden's professional opinion differed from that of the prosecution witnesses, as the psychiatrist suggested that Dryden might indeed be suffering from a mixed affective disorder, moderate to severe, possibly even amounting to an abnormality of mind. His notes attested to his belief that Dryden might well have been in a state of hysterical disassociation, a condition that occurs in situations of overwhelming anxiety and involves the division of the areas of mental and physical function and consciousness. In Mr Bowden's opinion, these considerations raised the issue of whether or not Dryden was in control of his physical actions at the time of the shooting, and he concluded that the defendant's mental ability at the time might well have been impaired substantially.

The complex and overwhelming body of evidence provided by the amassed psychologists and psychiatrists was later referred to by the judge in her summing up and no doubt featured largely in the jury's deliberations.

SEVENTEEN

I n any fictitious legal drama, from those of Perry Mason
to Rumpole of the Bailey's courtroom battles, the
dénouement of the case always comes in the counsels'
closing speeches. In the case of *Regina versus Albert Dryden*,
the drama had already been played out for the jury, frame
by frame. Now it was time for the barristers to use all their
considerable verbal deftness to draw together all the
various threads of testimony and weave them into
convincing arguments. It was then up to the jury to deliver
a verdict.

First, the prosecution counsel, John Milford, began his
closing speech. He argued that, despite Dryden's pleas of
not guilty to all the charges, there was incontrovertible
video evidence that undermined this claim. He also
reminded the jury that Dryden had, in his own testimony,

DEATH ON A SUMMER'S DAY

admitted to shooting Collinson and wounding Steven Campbell and Tony Belmont. He spoke of the conflicting medical evidence, whereby two of the psychiatrists who had appeared for the defence had diagnosed that Dryden had been suffering from a depressive mental illness that had rendered him with a substantially diminished sense of responsibility for the killing, contrasting this with Dr McClelland's judgement. 'He was no rubber band, suddenly finding himself stretched to the limit,' argued Milford. 'He was a man who had decided what he was going to do: to use a firearm.'

Milford made much of Dryden's threats to 'burn' Harry Collinson and of his sometimes violent history of conflict with the council. Dryden's preparatory actions on the day of the shooting were considered and deliberate, argued the lawyer; he had secreted the gun with the intention of using it, if necessary, which undermined the defence's position that Dryden had been provoked into killing Collinson. (Indeed, even Dryden's own lawyers had tried to convince him that, in order for this argument to have any chance of success, such provocation would have had to be life-threatening, which had clearly not been the case. As disturbing as the events of that day might have been for Dryden, his life had hardly been threatened.)

Again, Milford restated the prosecution's view that Dryden had acted in a pre-determined manner by replaying the section of videotape that captured Dryden's last warning to Collinson: 'It's entirely up to you, but you're making a sad decision.'

After a brief pause, Milford then went on to describe the series of shots that had killed Harry Collinson: 'That first bullet went mercilessly into Collinson's heart. Should there have been any doubt about its efficacy, a further two went into his vital organs. That, ladies and gentlemen, was murder.'

Milford returned to his seat to a deafening silence. Then all eyes were on the defence counsel, James Chadwin, who rose slowly and turned to address the jury. It was his task to plant reasonable doubt in the minds of its members, and he was under no illusions about how difficult that would be. Nonetheless, he did what he could to convince them that Dryden had done what he'd done under extreme provocation, comparing his defence of his property with the gritty defiance of a Wild West homesteader facing forcible eviction. With friends, journalists and a film crew looking on, he argued, Dryden could well have felt as if he was entering into a drama or acting out the part of a man pushed too far.

There was only a limited opportunity for Chadwin to dispute the factual testimony of all the witnesses, especially when such testimony was reinforced by the video evidence. After this, he could only hope that the weight of psychiatric evidence would fall in Dryden's favour, convincing the jury to deliver a verdict of not guilty of murder by means of diminished responsibility, resulting in a hospital order. Indeed, it's quite possible that, during the trial, the defence team attempted to persuade Dryden to change his plea, but it's more than likely that Dryden, obdurate and enjoying his day in court, didn't accept such sage advice.

Now the die was cast, however, and at 11.00 am on Monday, 30 March 1992, Mrs Justice Ebsworth began her summing-up of the case against Dryden, embarking on a speech that was to last for the rest of that day and half of the next. She gave a detailed summary of the evidence presented by both the defence and prosecution witnesses, placing great emphasis on the defences of provocation and diminished responsibility that had been put forward by Mr Chadwin, but balancing this by explaining the extent to which Dryden's responsibility might be considered to be diminished and what effect it might have on the jury's verdict. 'You have a straightforward difference in judgement between [the evidence of the psychiatrists],' she observed, 'and you have to evaluate that.'

She also reminded the jury that, in this particular case, they were in the unusual position of having video and photographic evidence to assist them in their deliberations, and pointed out that, while such evidence is common in cases of theft, it was rarely available in a murder case. In particular, she referred to instances in Dryden's interviews with Arthur Proud in which the defendant had demonstrated an awareness of his actions, and she cited many parts of Dryden's own testimony that demonstrated that he obviously had some recall of events, even being able to identify individuals who had climbed over the fence to get away from him as he began his rampage.

The jury was sent out to consider their verdict at 12.16pm on Tuesday, 31 March 1992, and they returned at 2:20pm – just two hours later. The foreman stood to deliver their verdict ('You could have heard a pin drop,' remembers Joe Williamson), then told the judge that they'd unanimously found Albert Dryden guilty of the murder of Harry Collinson, guilty of the attempted murder of Michael Dunstan and guilty of wounding Tony Belmont and Steven Campbell. As the verdict was read out, Dryden stood in the dock, eyes downcast and head bowed, and there were gasps from Dryden's supporters in the public gallery.

Once the initial reaction had subsided, the judge went on to give Dryden a sentence of life imprisonment for the murder of Harry Collinson and a concurrent sentence of life for the attempted murder of Michael Dunstan. She then meted out two further concurrent seven-year terms for the wounding of Tony Belmont and Steven Campbell. She made no recommendation as to the minimum sentence that Dryden should serve.

Judge Ebsworth pointed out to Dryden that, when the wrangle over his bungalow reached its tragic conclusion, it was 'entirely clear that the state of your mind on the day of the shooting was abnormal, but not sufficiently abnormal to diminish your responsibility for your actions. While the state of your mind remains as it was after June 20th – that is, disturbed and likely to react to stresses with which you coped in this grotesque way – you are a dangerous man. It is quite clear that those who are in control of you in prison will, of necessity, have to look at the state of your mind.'

Dryden was then led away down the steps in the dock, flanked by two court officials, to begin his life sentences.

EIGHTEEN

Once Dryden had been committed to prison, one would be forgiven for thinking that the people who had been touched by his murderous actions would have an opportunity to get some degree of closure and the chance to pick up the threads of their lives. Unfortunately, there were many strands to the story still to play out over the forthcoming years.

Two days after the verdict was handed down, Derwentside District Council announced that it would conduct an internal inquiry into the history of the planning dispute that had culminated in the murder of one of its employees, primarily in order to establish whether the actions of the council had been undertaken legitimately and in accordance with perceived best practice. 'We have nothing to hide,' said Alex Watson, the council leader at that time who, as a young man , had practised weight lifting with Dryden.

This inquiry yielded a well-structured report – written largely by Mike Bonser and endorsed by the council's chief executive, Neil Johnson – documenting the history of Dryden's relationships with the council, dating back to 1982. In the report, it was suggested that Harry Collinson's relationship with his killer might have clouded his judgement, and that perhaps if he'd adopted a more hardline approach from the outset his murder might have been avoided. The report went on to criticise the Department of the Environment for not informing Dryden that his last appeal against the demolition order was invalid. The council's chief executive acknowledged that the report could never be totally comprehensive, as some of the evidence was incomplete or ambiguous due to the length of the timescale and the large number of parties involved. Nonetheless, and despite certain assertions to the contrary, it appeared to be the only meticulous attempt to build a complete picture of what had happened.

In the report, Bonser accepted that it was likely that most councils would encounter difficult and potentially violent customers feeling hard done by, overlooked by officialdom and the system, noting that, as with that of Albert Dryden, such cases can prove to be amazingly complex and might stretch over a number of years.

The report also identified some imperfections within the council's own procedures, particularly regarding the need to establish a clear and transparent policy of communication and accountability. Safety, of course, was identified as a major issue, with notable comment made about the limited role played by the police in such circumstances and the possible need to employ other agencies, such as bailiffs, to act on the council's behalf.

The report's conclusion was that, overall, the authority had acted within the law and had at no time been 'capricious in its dealings with Mr Dryden', and that, despite having been required to work in an atmosphere of threats and violence, a commendably calm, professional and impartial approach had been adopted by the authority. The report was published on 4 June 1992 and was presented at a meeting attended by the full council, where it was accepted and later made available for public inspection.

Dryden's family and supporters greeted the report's publication with fury. They demanded a full public inquiry and continued to gather signatures for their petition requesting that Albert's convictions be reduced to those of manslaughter. This petition was then taken to London and was apparently delivered to Downing Street, although there remains some doubt about whether it was actually received there.

Meanwhile, Peter Donnelly, Dryden's brother-in-law, wrote a detailed eighteen-page response to the report's authors, and the supporters' group branded the report a 'whitewash'. 'I feel as if it's been manipulated and they've been economical with the truth,' complained Jill

Hall. 'Let's not just have the council's side; let's have everybody's side.'

In the press, council representatives dismissed such comments as errant nonsense, protesting that the report was as a 'warts and all' document and affirming that 'no stone had been left unturned'. Within the ranks of the elected members of council, however, one councillor – himself involved in a planning wrangle with his own authority – expressed his qualified support for Dryden's actions, while another – a longstanding friend of Dryden's – was much maligned for visiting him in prison.

Nevertheless, the council made it clear that they would co-operate fully if it was decided that there should be another, independent inquiry. Indeed, NALGO filed a request with the Health and Safety Executive for a public inquiry – preferably independent of both the police and the council – into the incident, in order to 'set the record straight', but their overtures were unsuccessful and it was felt that the council hadn't held the safety of its employees as being of 'paramount importance'.

In fact, the incident at Butsfield served to highlight the dangers that council officials often faced of both verbal and physical abuse. Joe Williamson recalls being shocked and surprised at reports that were trickling in from other union branches describing threats levelled at other planning officers. Apparently, one disgruntled applicant had even produced a shotgun and threatened to 'do a Dryden', while a man complaining about the state of footpaths in Gateshead made vague threats to councillors and claimed that he wasn't bluffing, 'just as Albert Dryden was not bluffing'.

Meanwhile, a farmer in Northumberland who was refused permission to build a bungalow for himself and his wife complained, 'I know how Dryden felt.' He then dumped six tonnes of manure on the doorstep of the local council offices. This man later received a scruffily written note from Dryden stating, 'I am proud of you.'

Some councils, like that of nearby Middlesbrough, did see fit to increase security for their officers and establish a register of dangerous clients. Derwentside District Council itself adopted a policy of ensuring that its staff never visited such individuals alone.

In April 1992, the Royal Town Planning Institute issued guidelines on personal safety for planners. The professional association – of which Harry Collinson was a member – felt the matter more keenly than most, and in its guidelines it acknowledged that the planning process was confrontational and that it could create 'tensions which may affect personal behaviour'. The guidelines contained several recommendations about the obligations of managers to protect their staff, about training and precautions necessary for site visits (notably that of requesting a police presence if appropriate) and about avoiding media attention.

In the event, no open public inquiry was ever held. Dryden's supporters' group continued in their efforts to have his sentences commuted. They hotly disputed the jury's verdict, protesting that Dryden had been tried unjustly, citing dozing jurors and colluding witnesses. They also tried to stage a meeting in the Civic Hall (adjacent to the council's offices, of all places), at which they planned to push for a further examination of the case. Not surprisingly, this rather insensitive request was firmly resisted by both staff and elected members of the council.

The demolition of the bungalow at Butsfield began quietly on 6 April 1992 when friends and relations of Dryden moved on to the land and started to take the building down, brick by brick. Albert's sister, Elsie, commented at the time, 'We just want it all to be over. I see the taking down of the bungalow as the final chapter. It has gone on and on and on. There has been tremendous strain on everyone.' Eventually, when the job was done, the hollow that Dryden had excavated was filled in, the land was restored and no trace of the bungalow remained, other than the brick archway under which Dryden had made his threats.

Immediately after the verdict had been handed down, Dryden had been discussing with his solicitor, Philip Jones, the possibility of an appeal against his conviction. Almost two years later, Dryden again appeared before the judiciary. A triumvirate of judges, headed by Lord Chief Justice Taylor, considered his appeal against his conviction on the grounds of provocation and diminished responsibility, but Lord Taylor decreed that, judging by the evidence submitted, it was overwhelmingly apparent that Dryden hadn't lost his self-control, despite his eccentric behaviour. The judges upheld the jury's decision and dismissed his appeal. As before, Dryden stood and listened

without emotion as the decision was announced. He
would later launch other, similarly unsuccessful attempts to
gain further hearings of his case.

Many who were there at Eliza Lane on the day of the
shooting were applauded for their courageous and
quick-thinking actions in the face danger. The three-
man BBC news team – reporter Tony Belmont,
soundman Simon Forrester and cameraman Phil
Dobson – were given a special award by the Royal
Television Society for outstanding bravery and
professionalism, with Tony being singled out for a special
commendation for continuing with his live report
despite being severely wounded. This wasn't the only
trophy he received; Arthur Proud also gave him the
bullet that the hospital team had removed from his arm.
Tony later had it made into a paperweight.

Later in 1991, *Northern Echo* photographer Michael
Peckett was voted North-East Journalist of the Year for his
pictures of the Dryden shooting. He later went on to win
numerous other prestigious national awards.

Within the police force, the three officers who had
secured Dryden's arrest received formal written
commendations from their chief constable, Frank Taylor, and
in addition John Taylor, Philip Brown and Andy Reay jointly
received the force's Matt Wilkinson Trophy, awarded annually
for acts of bravery. Taylor wrote in his citation that 'the trio
acted promptly in tackling a killer who could still have been
armed. They showed little regard for their own safety in a
difficult situation and acted in the service's highest tradition.'

Meanwhile, Derwentside District Council set up the Harry Collinson Memorial Fund, helped with financial contributions from Harry's friends and colleagues, to provide a memorial for its principal planning officer. The Fund served to endow the Harry Collinson Travel Scholarship at Newcastle University, Harry's *alma mater*, awarded annually to enable students to pursue projects on environmental topics in developing countries. As part of the conditions of the award, the scholarship holder may also be requested to attend a meeting held by Derwentside District Council, who may then assess the project undertaken, although it appears that no such meeting has ever been convened.

Bearing in mind Harry Collinson's interest in the environment, it wasn't difficult to choose an appropriate way of remembering him, and an area of woodland in Hamsterley of which he was particularly fond was dedicated as Harry's memorial, largely through the efforts an erstwhile colleague, Tom Stukins. This quiet piece of natural woodland is one of the last refuges of the red squirrel in northern England, and in the spring bluebells carpet the ground thickly. A plaque has been fixed to a large boulder within the wood to commemorate Harry's life. At first, the plaque was vandalised, and it was thought that Dryden's supporters were responsible for the damage, although this was never proved. The plaque is now well weathered and has become a part of the natural environment – just as Harry would have wanted it to be.

There were other later instances concerning the Dryden

case that erred on the dark side. The rock band Hawkwind were rumoured to be recording a song entitled 'Right To Decide' that had apparently been inspired by Dryden's actions, but a spokesman later said that, while the band did 'sympathise with Albert in his desperate stand against bloody-minded bureaucracy', they did not necessarily endorse his actions. After the adverse publicity, the record was quietly shelved. Dryden's friend George Cameron commented, 'None of us wants to glorify him. We don't want him to be a big hero.'

One of the more bizarre developments was a request from Dryden for the return of the Webley revolver with which he'd shot his victims. He'd refused to give up the weapon and sign a disclaimer permitting its destruction. When Chief Inspector Arthur Proud asked him why on earth he wanted to keep the gun, he revealed his plan to put it up for auction, expecting its sale to realise him tens of thousands of pounds. 'Because I carried that gun for forty years,' he argued, 'I feel I should be entitled to some money from it. The money could then be put into a savings account for me for when I come out of prison.'

Surprisingly, Dryden filed his application formally and it was heard in court before Mr Justice Waite on 10 July 1992. Predictably, however, it was strongly opposed by the Crown and his request was eventually denied. The pistol was ordered to be destroyed along with the rest of Dryden's formidable arsenal.

NINETEEN

Her Majesty's Prison Frankland is situated at the end of a housing estate on the outskirts of the city of Durham. At the time of its construction, it was one of the newer breed of state-of-the-art, high-security prisons that were springing up around the UK. Plain and efficient in design, behind its smooth, sheer, fawn-coloured walls – extending to its bombproof ramparts – reside some of the country's most dangerous criminals.

It was here that Albert Dryden began his life sentences. Even as a category A prisoner, he was a lot better off here than he'd been on remand in the antique jail in Durham, enjoying fewer restrictions. As he started his sentence, he tried to keep a low profile and after a while was allocated a gardening job, which suited him immensely.

I first met prisoner CK 0635, Albert Dryden, at

Frankland on Wednesday, 12 September 1998, over six years after his initial imprisonment. The only other time that I'd ever seen him was on the day of his arrest, and that had been from a distance as he was being restrained outside the caravan.

I visited Dryden there at his invitation, along with his brother-in-law, Peter Donnelly, and Jill Hall, who had been a stalwart member of his supporters' campaign, who had both sought Dryden's consent after I'd discussed with them my proposal to write a book about the shooting and subsequent trial. I was included on the visiting order. Previously, I'd visited such establishments only in a professional capacity, where formalities had been kept to a minimum, and it came as something of a shock when I was searched, fingerprinted and herded into a cage with all the other visitors, to be comprehensively sniffed by a drugs dog. Most of my personal possessions were removed and placed in a locker for safe keeping, to be returned to me on my way out.

Eventually, Peter, Jill and I were called through to the visiting hall, where comfortable, airport-style seats were laid out in blocks of four low coffee tables. Three of the seats in each block were blue, designated for visitors, and one was yellow, for the prisoner. From where I was sitting, facing down the visiting hall, I watched as Dryden, carrying a roll of paper, was conducted in by a prison officer and brought to his seat. I recognised him immediately from the news coverage, although his appearance had changed considerably since his trial —

stocky, short, mid-fifties, with collar-length white hair combed across his head to hide his baldness. He had a rubicund complexion above a white spiky beard and watery blue eyes that were never still, darting around the room, watching everything that was going on. He looked, in fact, a little like a cheap in-store Father Christmas having a bad day.

As soon as he had sat down, Albert began to complain to the prison officers about the seat he'd been allocated. His back was to a radiator, which would irritate his skin condition, he said, and he threatened to see the medical officer the following morning and complain to the governor about his treatment if they didn't move him. The prison officers were obviously familiar with such a display, as he was told in no uncertain terms to sit down and get on with his visit or he would be returned to his cell. His complaining ceased, though he carried on grumbling under his breath.

Once I'd been briefly introduced, I was largely ignored for a long while, although I was aware that Dryden was casting wary glances in my direction. He seemed to accept my presence, though, while Peter brought him up to date with the family gossip. After a while, Albert picked up his roll of paper, laid it on the table, delicately smoothed it out and explained to Peter and Jill that he'd been taking painting classes, and that this was his latest creation. It had been admired by his art teacher, he reported proudly, who had apparently told him that he was an accomplished artist. I could distinguish that it was some sort of bird, but it seemed to be an extremely poor impressionistic representation of one, something like the crayon scribblings of a child.

After this offering had been duly admired, Peter turned to me and told Dryden about my plan to write a book about the circumstances that led to his incarceration and help to put the record straight. Jill put in that I'd interviewed her, and told Dryden that I seemed trustworthy, which seemed to reassure him somewhat. We had a cup of tea and I began to tell him who I was and what I was doing, but before I'd got very far Dryden interrupted me and proceeded to tell us all about the grounds he believed he had for a further appeal, then launched into a vehement castigation of the corrupt judges within the legal system.

Dryden became more and more enthusiastic about the idea of my writing a book about him, however, which he thought might help him in his quest for an appeal. I protested that all I was intending to do was write a true account of the events surrounding Harry Collinson's death, although, I allowed, there might be a few questions in the book that might shed a different light on matters. He appeared to accept that as a starting premise and seemed to be quite willing to help me.

As for Dryden's hope for another appeal, the fact of the matter was that he'd exhausted all the avenues of appeal long ago. The facts themselves were unequivocal, captured on camera. Nonetheless, he was convinced that his case would end up on the Home Secretary's desk, and even at the European Court of Human Rights. In this, Dryden's thinking struck an interesting parallel to his dispute with Derwentside District Council, which took on a scale disproportionate to its subject.

Dryden was still obsessed with the unfair planning process that led up to the shooting, relatively unconcerned about the incident itself. Whenever I tried to ask specific questions about what had happened on 20 June 1991, he would bring the conversation back to his own plight as the hard-done-by little man just trying to 'do his own thing', without causing harm to anyone. It wasn't until later much that I realised that prevarication could have represented a conscious effort by Dryden to avoid admitting responsibility for the murder itself.

Dryden railed at some length against the unfairness of the prison regime, which to him was just another aspect of the authority that had ground him down all his life. Referring to his fellow prisoners as murderers, thugs, rapists and terrorists, he didn't appear to have any comprehension of why he was in prison or of the fact that he was himself a murderer. He seemed preoccupied with his health and how difficult it was to get a bath (he wasn't fond of the available showers).

From what I could gather, Dryden was prone to getting into confrontations with fellow prisoners. He told us that, one time, he was sharing the prison gym with some black prisoners who were exercising to loud music. After they ignored a number of his requests to turn the volume down, he walked over and switched off the radio – and was then assaulted by his fellow prisoners, narrowly escaping serious injury before being rescued by the prison staff. He had numerous other tales of similar mistreatment, at the hands of both his fellow inmates and prison officers, who he thought were trying to poison him. The problem was that he demonstrated such a complex and not very subtle mix of bigotry, pedantry and obsessiveness that it was hardly surprising that he might suffer at the hands of others. If such traits hadn't proved to be so dangerous, Dryden's Walter Mitty-style approach to life might even have been moderately endearing.

As we left Dryden and recovered our belongings, I didn't feel that I'd achieved much, although I was pleased to have made initial contact with him, no matter how distracted he'd been. Peter believed that the visit had been a great leap forward, however, as Dryden had previously had no truck with any of the other journalists or writers who had asked to see him.

When I got back, I wrote to Dryden, sending him some stamps and phone cards and telling him more about my plan to write a book about him. Between that time and that of my next visit, on 13 July 1999, we corresponded by post and occasionally by telephone. By that time, he'd been downgraded to a category B prisoner and moved to Garth Prison in Preston, Lancashire. This time, I visited him with his sister, Elsie, and intended to bring someone with me who would take notes, although this plan was thwarted when we found out we weren't allowed to bring any writing materials into the visiting area.

As he walked into the visiting area that day, Dryden raised his hand and greeted me like an old friend. Then, as soon as he'd sat down, and much to the irritation of his sister, he launched into a diatribe against the supposedly biased Tariff Board, who had recently refused to consider a reduction in his sentence. Most of his spleen was directed at someone named Mr Khan, a member of the Board who'd written to him, and Dryden leaped on his ethnic origin as a reason for his intransigence and his inability to agree with Dryden's own point of view.

Once I'd finally got him off this subject, Dryden was only too happy to recount past events. He seemed to have an encyclopaedic knowledge of dates, times and places, but whether these were accurate was unconfirmed. He talked about his childhood and his family with fondness (although he was prone to boast about his own abilities), while, on the subject of guns, he said that he read everything about them that he could get his hands on. (It was on this occasion that he told me the story of how he acquired the .455 Webley – still bemoaning its loss – and how he'd manufactured his own bullets and built and adapted guns.) Leaning forward conspiratorially, he whispered, 'All the warders here think I'm fascinated by guns. I saw a western one Saturday lunchtime. Somebody was using a .2003 Winchester. I heard one screw whispering to another, "Should we let him watch that? Should he be watching that?"'

Dryden then went on to recall his time at the steelworks in Consett and spoke of drinking cans of beer on the night shift and cooking casseroles on the furnace. He told of the red dust which formed 'a sort of balloon over Consett' and of how the houses' windows and the washing on the lines would be stained ochre. He could still tell a good story.

More ominously, Dryden told of the letters of support that he continued to receive from a surprisingly large number of people wanting to be associated with him, looking for the cachet of corresponding with a killer. There was even a letter from a county sheriff in Montana, who expressed some sympathy with his situation. The sheriff's nephew, who was apparently working at Cape Canaveral, had also written to Dryden, inviting him over when he got out of prison (no doubt to offer his advice to NASA – who, incidentally, had apparently told him that his own version of rocket fuel was still being used to power the rockets of today). Despite repeated attempts on my part, however, Dryden still refused to speak directly about the murder, rapidly changing the subject each time I introduced it.

The last time I saw Albert Dryden was at Garth Prison on 18 April 2000. That day, he was preoccupied with a possible move to Nottingham Prison. He was pleased, as he was dissatisfied with Garth Prison – just as he was dissatisfied with his solicitors and with the fact that it didn't seem his request for another appeal was being processed. At times, he was almost incomprehensible, speaking in staccato bursts. His hair was askew, his beard had been cropped and his eyes were rheumy. I tried to steer the conversation towards the circumstances regarding his offence, but, exasperatingly, he would inevitably return to the subject of his perpetual persecution at the hands of authority. When I asked him directly if he was sorry that he'd killed Harry Collinson, a crafty, wary look came into his eyes and he quickly changed the subject.

After about two hours, neither of us had anything left to say to the other. I bid him farewell and left.

Eventually, after a protracted correspondence with the Home Office and Garth, the prison's governor informed me that I was authorised to conduct a tape-recorded interview with Dryden inside the prison, and that Dryden had consented. I was elated, as this was something of a coup.

Hoping to give Dryden the chance to address those subjects that I felt we'd been avoiding, I prepared a list of questions, which I sent to him in prison. The list spooked him, forced him into a position where he'd finally have to confront those issues he'd been avoiding for so many years, and provoked a very angry phone call and his eventual refusal to see me again. Since that time, I wrote to him on two further occasions but heard nothing – from Dryden, at least; I was rebuffed by a terse solicitor's letter informing me that he refused to speak to me ever again.

Dryden continues to fight against authority, convinced of his own rectitude. He is a prodigious correspondent and has worn out at least five firms of solicitors and one barrister, many of which he claims are in league with the Crown. He is a highly suggestible individual who is prone to exploitation by the unscrupulous. He features on many websites, both here and in the USA, and is unfairly mentioned in articles with mass-murderers such as Fred West, Charles Manson and even Jack the Ripper. He is represented often as a wronged and oppressed minority figure, and as usual his claims are wild and exaggerated. It has been alleged on his behalf, for instance, again without foundation, that at the time of his arrest, the then chief constable of Durham and Harry Collinson were regular golfing partners and that Dryden himself was the victim of a huge Masonic plot designed to keep him in prison, involving various figures in positions of authority, including all council officials, police and prison staff, the entire legal profession (including his own legal team), the jury at his trial and even up to the Home Secretary.

The truth is that Harry Collinson had never shown any interest in golf and certainly hadn't contemplated joining any Masonic institution, as this would have been against his socialist beliefs.

Largely as a result of such correspondence, Dryden has become the focus of attention for some bizarre cults who thrive on information about convicted murderers, the bloodier the better. Contact with these groups and other individuals has fed Dryden's ego to the extent that he believes he has gathered a substantial band of influential supporters who will eventually secure his release.

Indeed, there is evidence that Dryden is becoming increasingly divorced from reality, such as his conviction that there is a conspiracy within the prison service to withhold his mail, torture him by subjecting him to a series of rigged intelligence and assessment tests and, eventually, kill him by poisoning his food. In fact, every effort has been made to accommodate Dryden, even to the extent of moving him to Holme House Prison in Cleveland so that he could be closer to his family and friends (although he was later returned to Nottingham as the new prison's regime didn't suit him). He is described as argumentative and sulky, with an exaggerated sense of his own importance, constantly asserting that his current dilemma is not of his own making but is the fault of others.

Tellingly, it wasn't until the possibility of a parole hearing was first mooted, when he was later transferred to Rye Hill Prison, Warwickshire, that he ever showed any remorse for the death of Harry Collinson. Many think that he has done his time but Harry's brother, Roy, is firmly of the opinion that he should 'rot in jail'.

By October 2003, Dryden was sufficiently aware of the necessity for him to demonstrate his remorse to a Parole Board that he wrote to the Newcastle *Evening Chronicle*, confessing how sorry he was for what he'd done.

By January 2004, it was revealed that Dryden was compiling yet another dossier regarding his mistreatment behind bars and the injustices that had been meted out to him. A year later, he was transferred again, this time to Haverigg Prison in Cumbria, which he saw as one step further towards his release. If and when he is eventually let out, Dryden will remain on licence for the rest of his life. Should he ever transgress again, he'll be sent straight back to prison.

EPILOGUE

The murder of Harry Collinson by Albert Dryden touched the lives of many people, both near and distant, and a great many words have been said and written about the tragedy. Those words cannot and should not be refined; they must be left for posterity, so that history may judge whether mistakes were made, whether the debacle could have been avoided or whether the aftermath was handled correctly.

Who was to blame for the killing, and why? Obviously, Dryden carried out the act, but there were many contributory factors that should not be disregarded. Questions must be asked of both Derwentside District Council and the police. Why were events allowed to reach such a pitch?

Why wasn't the building of the bungalow stopped earlier?

Why was Dryden not recognised as being dangerous?

Why, after the event, did he command such a groundswell of support?

What happened to Garry Willey's telephone call? Was it just lost or, in reality, disregarded?

Why, if there was no danger, were firearms officers involved?

Why was no tactical adviser ever consulted?

How did things get so far out of hand? Was it due to incompetence, mismanagement, plain stupidity or sheer misfortune?

Why was no proper forum ever provided in which these issues could be discussed openly?

Differing views paint Dryden, on the one hand, as an oppressed hero struggling against authority and, on the other, as a cold-blooded murderer deserving only the final sanction of the death penalty. This book offers no answers; it merely poses the questions. The rest is left to others.

'I cleared out Harry's desk, took his long white raincoat that he habitually wore, and, from his desk, I took his bait box, still full of his sandwiches for that day.'

'The police's job is to prevent a thing — that's first and foremost, as I understand it. They didn't have control over the situation. They didn't appear to feel threatened when Dryden produced the revolver. They were too far away to take any action. They were too far away to do anything when he pointed the gun at Harry. They weren't close enough to do anything, to do the Dixon of Dock Green *bit.'*

'*Albert had reacted to the situation rather than acted. I don't think that he mentally chose to go down and shoot this man deliberately; I felt that something had gone in his mind.*'

'*I was thinking about the man's family. I was very upset that I was looking at someone who had been killed, and I couldn't understand why he had been killed.*'

'*How many people go into a job in local government anticipating that they might die? If you join the Army, there's always the possibility, and I suppose if you're a fireman there's a possibility, but I think for local government officers it's a pretty remote chance.*'

'*God help him if we ever meet him. I would dearly love to see him hang. I would have sprung the trap myself and I would have lent them the rope.*'

'*I think it changed the approach by police officers to firearms incidents that followed. It wasn't, "Pooh, pooh. It'll never happen now." It brought home that, because you wear a blue suit with shiny buttons, you're not invincible; you're not Superman, and you can get shot.*'

'*He said, "It is going to be really funny, because I've got a dummy hand grenade and I'm going to roll it underneath the digger and see them fly." We didn't believe he was going to do it.*'

'It's just awful that it could have happened, but I think that the whole situation put people into extreme positions where they'd been backed into corners, both Harry and Albert Dryden. I mean, Harry still wasn't taking it seriously, quite obviously. He didn't really think that Albert Dryden would take this to its ultimate conclusion.'

'To sum him up, the first thing I would say about Albert Dryden would be that he was a cold-blooded killer. In the same breath, when you look over his life, it has been quite sad.'

It should never have happened.

APPENDIX

DURHAM CONSTABULARY

DERWENTSIDE SUBDIVISION
OPERATIONAL ORDER

DERWENTSIDE DISTRICT COUNCIL AND
ALBERT DRYDEN

Derwentside District Council have commenced an operation against Albert DRYDEN, 6 Priestman Avenue, The Grove, Consett, for failing to comply with an Enforcement Notice relating to buildings at Eliza Lane, Butsfield, Consett (see Appendix 'A').

Under Section 178 of the Town and Country Planning Act 1990, the Council are now entitled to enter this land

and carry out steps stated in the Enforcement Notice, which, in this case, are the removal of <u>two</u> of the buildings.

A demolition company has been contracted to carry out this removal at 9am, Thursday, 20 June 1991. It is expected to take two hours to complete the task.

INTENTION

Our aim is to:

Prevent any breach of the peace taking place;

To supervise the free movement of traffic along the A68 road and Eliza Lane/Green Lane junction.

It is anticipated that that part of Eliza Lane running from the A68 to Green Lane junction will be closed to all traffic.

METHOD

A briefing will take place at Consett Police office at 8.15am on Thursday, 20 June 1991.

Personnel will be deployed by 8.30am the same day.

DAVID BLACKIE

PERSONNEL		
Inspector 1395 YOUNG	–	Officer in charge
Acting Sgt. 1049 HUGHES PC 523 PIERCY	–	Responsible for closure of Eliza Lane and supervising the free movement of traffic on adjoining roads. Vehicle I 15.
Sergeant 2273 CAMPBELL PC 507 CAMPBELL PC 520 KIRKUP	–	Will accompany Derwentside District Council personnel and demolition contractor to the scene. Vehicle H 03.
PC 1956 STOKOE	–	To accompany OIC. Vehicle I 12.
Sergeant 1812 BARTLETT (Durham Sub-Divisional Personnel)	–	To standby at Consett Police office. Vehicle I 04.
UOD Traffic Branch	–	Armed-response vehicle available for deployment, if required.
Acting Sgt 789 BRIDGE UOD dog section	–	To stand by at Consett Police office.
Ambulance Service	–	Paramedic to stand by at Consett Police office

Movement of personnel to the scene will be by Castleside and A68 road.

Any prisoners will be brought to Consett Police Station. Précis of evidence to be completed before dismissal.

It is anticipated that DRYDEN will have up to three friends present on the site. Local press and television are aware of the situation and will be in attendance at the scene. Force press officer has been informed but will not be in attendance at the scene.

DRYDEN is an unpredictable character who has made numerous threats in the past. He was recently arrested for criminal damage and an assault on the council enforcement officer.

ADMINISTRATION		
Dress	–	Present day uniform with light raincoats, if necessary. Appointments will be carried.
Refreshments	–	Contingency plans will be implemented if and when the situation demands.
Transport prisoners	–	I 04 and/or H 03 will be used for transporting prisoners.
Dismissal	–	If appropriate, debriefing of the operation will take place at Consett Police office. Officers to be stood down by Inspector YOUNG when deemed appropriate.

COMMUNICATIONS

All officers will be in possession of personal radios tuned to channel 30. Strict radio procedure will be observed and

DAVID BLACKIE

directed by Communications Staff at Consett Police Office. VHF radio to be used only in EMERGENCY.

HQ control room are aware of the operation.

Inspector 1395 YOUNG